CLASSIC TEXTS IN
MUSIC EDUCATION 16

# SUBSTANCE OF SEVERAL COURSES OF LECTURES ON MUSIC

# CLASSIC TEXTS IN MUSIC EDUCATION

General Editor of the Series
BERNARR RAINBOW MEd PhD

Wm Crotch

# Substance
# of Several Courses of
# Lectures on Music

(1831)

Introduced by
BERNARR RAINBOW

Reproduced under the direction
of Leslie Hewitt for
BOETHIUS PRESS

Additional Material
© 1986 Boethius Press Limited
Clarabricken, Co Kilkenny
Ireland
and
Bernarr Rainbow

British Library Cataloguing in Publication Data

Crotch, William
    Substance of several courses of lectures on
    music (1831). — (Classic texts in music
    education; 16)
    1. Music
    I. Title
    780   ML160

    ISBN 0-86314-114-5

The publishers thank
Dr Bernarr Rainbow for lending
his copy for reprinting

Printed by Boethius Press
Clarabricken, Co Kilkenny
Ireland

# INTRODUCTION

When William Crotch was appointed Professor of Music at Oxford in 1797 at the early age of 22 the formal duties of the post were traditionally limited to composing choral Odes to mark particular occasions, examining candidates for degrees in music, and playing the organ at certain university ceremonies. Already organist of one of the college chapels, like most of his immediate predecessors in the Chair, Crotch also encouraged and organised secular musical activities besides directing the concerts given by the Music Room orchestra. But soon after his appointment, unlike former professors, he instituted a course of lectures on music within the university. There was as yet no formal undergraduate course of tuition in music in the modern sense; Crotch explained that he had made his object 'an endeavour to raise the taste'. These innovatory lectures, illustrated by the Music Room orchestra and his own performance on the piano, were designed for general audiences and were moreover the first of their kind.

Crotch was equally a pioneer in another respect. The extensive range of musical examples drawn largely from his own library and performed to illustrate his lectures was arranged by him in keyboard transcription and published under the title *Specimens of Various Styles of Music*. The three folio volumes concerned comprised a prototype historical anthology of unfamiliar music designed to widen the serious music lover's acquaintance with the repertoire and idioms of former times. And while the summaries of Crotch's lectures which form the substance of the present volume were not themselves published until 1831, the companion *Specimens* were first issued more than twenty years earlier. Several new editions followed, the last being in 1845; and throughout the nineteenth century Crotch's *Specimens* were to provide the most extensive selection of early music available for domestic and student use.

Crotch's efforts to earn for music a respected place in academic circles at Oxford heralded a century of intermittent progress toward its general acceptance as a modern academic discipline.

But while the tradition lingered that music was not a pursuit worthy of a gentleman—a prejudice that the current lack of general education among most professional musicians then did nothing to combat—it required the intervention of a musician of unusually wide accomplishments even to question accepted opinion.

His childhood and youth had equipped Crotch well for the task. An infant prodigy whose phenomenal gifts were reported to the Royal Society after he had been summoned at the age of three to play before the king and queen, he had then been taken on tour throughout Britain. By the age of eleven he could play the piano, organ and violin, and had begun to compose, besides showing a genuine talent for drawing and painting. Next followed two years as assistant to the Professor of Music at Cambridge where Crotch regularly accompanied the services on the organ at King's, Trinity and the university church. Then in 1788 the need to make good his general education was pressed and he became the protégé of one of the tutors at Magdalen College, Oxford, who began to prepare him for matriculation and ordination. Two years later this goal was abandoned when his elderly mentor's health failed; and instead in 1790 Crotch was appointed organist of Christ Church, Oxford, at the age of fifteen. He took the degree of B Mus four years later and succeeded Dr Hayes as Professor in 1797.

There can be little doubt that the years after 1786 that Crotch spent in constant proximity to undergraduates much his own age not only influenced his intellectual and cultural development, but also persuaded him that an attempt to combat the musical ignorance of these young men was a task worth undertaking. Aware of Sir John Hawkins' declaration that one of his aims in compiling his *History* was 'to remove the numberless prejudices respecting music, which only those entertain who are ignorant of the science',[1] Crotch clearly addressed his lectures to general audiences with the same end in view.

But Crotch was eventually to grow disappointed at the lack of support which his musical endeavours received from the university authorities, and, in 1804, when he was invited to speak in future

1. J. Hawkins, *General History of the Science & Practice of Music*, 1776, edn of 1853, vol. I, p. xvii

at the Royal Institution in London, the Oxford lectures were discontinued. Thereafter his active connection with Oxford progressively weakened. The metropolis offered greater musical opportunity than the conservatively narrow university, and in 1806 Crotch resigned his post as organist of Christ Church and moved to London permanently. Residence was not then required of the Professor of Music, the salary a miserable £12 a year; and though returning to Oxford only when formal duties demanded his attendance there, Crotch continued to hold the Chair until his death in 1847. Soon established as a leading musical figure in the capital, during the next twenty years he became celebrated in turn as performer, composer, teacher, writer and scholar. Upon its foundation in 1822 he was appointed the first Principal of the Royal Academy of Music.

Influential though the treatises on Harmony and Composition which he published unquestionably were, Crotch's most important contribution was made in his lecture-recitals. The series begun in Oxford at the turn of the century was continued in London until 1832, several of the original texts still surviving in manuscript in the Record Office in Norwich,[2] his birthplace, in addition to those summarised by him in the present volume. The importance of these lectures lay not only in their novelty as the first to be delivered on musical history in Britain; at least as important was their influence in extending to musical thought the current practice of drawing illustrative and evaluative analogies between different branches of the fine arts.

A man of exceptionally wide interests whose writings covered fields so diverse as architecture and astronomy, geometry and pyrotechnics, Crotch was also a talented painter who habitually carried a box of watercolours with him on his daily occasions. It is not difficult to see in his liking for drawing and painting the factor that encouraged him to model his own lectures upon Sir Joshua Reynolds' *Discourses* on the visual arts. Indeed, his pages are liberally interspersed with quotations from Reynolds. And from the *Discourses* it was but a step to the writings of Edmund Burke and Uvedale Price who had established the terminology which

2. Norfolk and Norwich Record Office, *file nos* 11063-67 and 11228-33

divided style in the visual arts into three categories: the Sublime, the Beautiful, and the Picturesque. The usage had dominated aesthetic theory in eighteenth-century England,[3] and was now adopted by Crotch to distinguish between different types of composition in his own system of musical appraisal.

A less obvious, far less important, but perhaps equally revealing aspect of Crotch's addiction to analogy between the arts is to be found in his choice of title when publishing the musical excerpts used to illustrate his lectures. As an enthusiastic student of architecture he was familiar with the massive volumes of engraved plates recently published to represent various styles of architecture. John Carter's *Specimens* was a celebrated example. That Crotch should have chosen to publish his keyboard transcriptions of *Specimens of Various Styles of Music* with so reminiscent a title will hardly have been coincidental.

Moreover, circumstances had encouraged Crotch to seek affinities between the fine arts during his formative years. On his arrival in Oxford while still a boy he had soon encountered a sympathetic spirit in the ex-patriot German violinist who was leader of the Music Room orchestra. Like Crotch, John Malchair (Johann Malscher) was also a gifted watercolour artist, and the two became friends though Malchair was then almost sixty years old. In his lectures Crotch was later to recall how Malchair had likened the concertos of Corelli to the landscapes of Claude Lorraine: 'Each was a perfect whole considered by itself, but in a collection of them there was but little variety.'[4] During Crotch's years in Oxford conversations with Malchair must often have run along such lines.

It was through the influence of Malchair, too, that young Crotch first developed an interest in traditional and folk music—'a subject hitherto considered of but little importance... which I am not disposed to view in that light.'[5] Malchair had made the collection and study of 'national and other curious music' a favourite pursuit, and Crotch acknowledged that the

3. W. J. Hipple, Jr, *The Beautiful, the Sublime, & the Picturesque in Eighteenth-century Aesthetic Theory*, Carbondale, Ill., 1957

4. *op. cit*, p. 108

5. *Specimens*, vol. 1, pp. 13-14

unexpectedly large number of examples of such music contained in the first volume of his *Specimens* was assembled with Malchair's assistance.

Just how far Crotch's enthusiasm for the music of the past merely paralleled the Gothick sympathies of *cognoscenti* in the other arts can be allowed to remain a matter for debate. Quoted in isolation certain of his critical judgments may be used to condemn him as reactionary. But read in their due context even his most severe strictures upon what he saw as contemporary malpractice prove to be directed only against vulgarity and lack of dignity in music designed for use in a religious setting. Far from prizing antiquity for its own sake Crotch held it a common error to suppose that antiquity alone created the veneration felt for ancient church music.

For William Crotch the musical world of his youth had been divided into two opposing factions—'the one despising the trifling melodies of the opera, and the other the barbarous and mechanical structures of the fugue.'[6] His mature view of the matter was that during his lifetime those factions were at length reconciled when Mozart, 'the greatest of all modern composers', demonstrated by his effective use of counterpoint that 'science could no longer be held in ridicule'.[7] Crotch believed the public taste of the nation was in a gradual state of improvement and had reached a higher standard than it had known for half a century. The *Substance of Several Courses of Lectures on Music* conducts the modern reader on an excursion through the first decades of the nineteenth century to form his own estimate.

6. *op. cit*, p. 148-49
7. *op. cit*, p. 149

# THE ROYAL INSTITUTION

Founded by Sir Benjamin Thompson, Baron von Rumford (1753-1814) an American-born philanthropist and inventor, and first announced in his *Proposals* of 1799. Its objectives as there stated were to be two-fold: first, the diffusion of the knowledge of new improvements; secondly, teaching the application of science to the useful purpose of life. A charter was obtained in 1799 and building began in Albemarle Street on plans designed by the founder.

An account of a visit to the Royal Institution not long after its foundation is contained in the correspondence of an American visitor to London in 1805:

The Institution was set on foot a few years ago for the purpose of encouraging useful knowledge in general and for facilitating the introduction of useful mechanical improvements. Now, public lectures are delivered in the institution on different branches of science, and particularly on natural philosophy and chemistry. The establishment was munificently endowed [by subscription] and Count Rumford placed at its head…A number of contiguous houses in Albemarle Street have been so connected as to form one building and this contains the numerous apartments of the Royal Institution. There are rooms for reading the journals and newspapers; others, devoted to the library, which is already considerably extensive; others to the philosophical apparatus, the lectures, the minerals, the professors, the cookery, servants, etc…The theatre is the room where the lectures are given. It is a superb apartment, and fitted up with great convenience. It is semicircular, and contains a pit and gallery, in which the seats rise row behind row. It is lighted from above, through a circular orifice, which, whenever the lecturer wishes to darken the room, can be shut at pleasure by a horizontal screen connected with a cord. This theatre has often contained a thousand persons. It is so fashionable a resort, that the ladies of Westminster are in the habit of coming to the Royal Institution to derive instruction from the rational pursuits of philosophy…But as one object of the institution has been to attract an audience, of course everything has worn a popular air, and the amusing and the brilliant have been studiously pursued as well as the useful.

From Benjamin Silliman, *A Journal of Travels in England, Holland and Scotland* (New Haven, 1820) quoted in H. S. Commager, *Britain through American Eyes* (Bodley Head, 1974), pp. 59-61.
Additional details from the *Dictionary of National Biography* (Compact Edn., 1975)

# SUBSTANCE

OF

## SEVERAL COURSES

OF

# LECTURES ON MUSIC,

READ IN THE UNIVERSITY OF OXFORD, AND

IN THE METROPOLIS.

---

By WILLIAM CROTCH, Mus. D.

PROFESSOR OF MUSIC, OXFORD; AND PRINCIPAL OF THE ROYAL
ACADEMY OF MUSIC, LONDON.

---

LONDON:

PRINTED FOR

LONGMAN, REES, ORME, BROWN, AND GREEN,

PATERNOSTER-ROW.

1831.

LONDON :
Printed by A. & R. Spottiswoode,
New-Street-Square.

# CONTENTS.

## ERRATA.

Page 60. line 11. for " Fata," read " Fate."

—— 100. lines 2. & 8. } for " Green," read " Greene."
—— 109. line 14.

——— 109. note †, for " Ibid. pp. 29. 123." read " pp. 22. 100."

——— 115. note, for " 17." read " 7. 12."

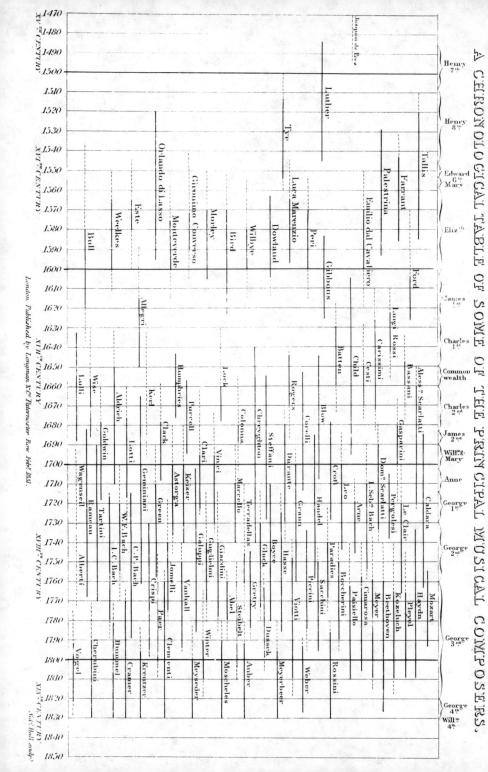

A CHRONOLOGICAL TABLE OF SOME OF THE PRINCIPAL MUSICAL COMPOSERS.

London, Published by Longman & Co Paternoster Row Feb.y 1831.

Sid.t Hall sculp.t

# LECTURES ON MUSIC.

## CHAP. I.

### INTRODUCTORY.

Music is both an art and a science. As a
science, it includes the theories of sound and of
musical composition; but, in the following definition, the word science signifies the theory of
sound only.

" Music " (says Sir William Jones) " belongs,
" as a science, to an interesting part of natural
" philosophy, which, by mathematical deduc-
" tions from constant phenomena, explains the
" causes and properties of sound, limits the
" number of sounds to a certain series, which

" perpetually recurs, and fixes the ratio which
" they bear to each other, or to one leading
" term : but, considered as an art, it combines
" the sounds which philosophy distinguishes, in
" such a manner as to gratify our ears, or affect
" our imaginations ; or, by uniting both objects,
" to captivate the fancy, while it pleases the
" sense ; and, speaking, as it were, the language
" of nature, to raise corresponding ideas and
" connections in the mind of the hearer. It
" then, and then only, becomes what we call a
" fine art, allied very nearly to poetry, painting,
" and rhetoric. Thus, it is the province of the
" philosopher to discover the true direction and
" divergence of sound propagated by the suc-
" cessive compressions and expansions of air, as
" the vibrating body advances and recedes ; to
" show why sounds themselves may excite a
" tremulous motion in particular bodies ; to de-
" monstrate the law by which all the particles of
" air, when it undulates with great quickness, are
" continually accelerated and retarded ; to com-
" pare the number of pulses in agitated air with
" that of the vibrations which cause them; to

" compute the velocities and intervals of those
" pulses in atmospheres of different density and
" elasticity; to account, as well as he can, for
" the affections which music produces; and,
" generally, to investigate the causes of the
" many wonderful appearances which it exhi-
" bits: but the artist, without considering, and
" even without knowing, any of the sublime
" theorems in the philosophy of sound, may at-
" tain his end by a happy selection and judicious
" application of melody, harmony, rhythm, and
" modulation." *

The science of music will not constitute the
subject of the present work. A few lectures
were once, indeed, written and delivered on
the theory of sound, and on musical composition, by the author, at the request of some of
his auditors; but as his classes never consisted,
at the University or the Metropolis, wholly, or
even principally, of philosophers or composers,
but rather of lovers of music, performers, and
perhaps a few young composers, the lecturer has

* Sir W. Jones's Essays.

generally made his principal object an endeavour to improve the taste.

The study, however, of the science of music is strongly recommended to every lover of the art. The theory of musical sound may be turned to much practical account. This determines the exact mode of tuning, and teaches the nature of temperament, or the distribution of unavoidable imperfection; it demonstrates the perfection of the human voice, and shows the relative excellence of the various instruments. Thus, the human voice is called perfect, because, excepting as to its compass, it knows no limit to the number of its sounds; its accordance is perfect. Some instruments approach towards a perfect intonation; the violin, tenor, and violoncello, as long as they are stopped by the fingers, without using the open strings, may be perfectly in tune; but, as this cannot continue long, imperfection creeps in. Both keyed and wind instruments have a limited number of sounds in each octave; usually twelve; a number too small to admit of perfect tuning in more than one or two out of the unlimited number of modes in general use. A slight inspection of the Monochord, or Harmonical Canon of Pythagoras *, will show the relative lengths of string necessary to produce the sounds required, and make the necessity of temperament apparent. Equal temperament is so called, because the imperfection is equally distributed among the twelve fifths, the other intervals becoming equally imperfect by consequence; unequal temperament improves some keys at the expense of others. Various have been the attempts to diminish imperfection by increasing the number of sounds in an octave. Many wind instruments, as the flute, oboe, clarionet, and bassoon, have had the number of their apertures greatly increased, which, with the management of the breath of the performer, render these instruments superior, as to the accuracy of their intonation, to the organ or pianoforte. Sliding mouth-pieces have, for the same purpose, been affixed to the trumpet and horn. Keys added to the bugle-horn have rendered the most simple of all instruments capable of

* See Elements of Musical Composition, by the Author.

performing the most refined melody — that which had only five notes, (the same harmonics as are produced with any simple tube, as the perforated horn of an animal,) is now one of the most pleasing of military instruments. Amongst the improvements on keyed instruments, we may notice the addition of notes in Father Smith's organ at the Temple church, in the harpsichords of Dr. Smith of Cambridge, in the organs of Clagget and Hawkes, and in the piano-fortes of Löeschman. The approach to perfection in all these was in proportion to the number of notes added to each octave; and, of course, the bulk, inconvenience, and expense of the instrument, and the difficulty of tuning it, were increased in the same proportion. It seems highly probable, therefore, that we must remain contented with twelve sounds in an octave on our keyed instruments. But which should we use, the equal or unequal temperament?

The reply to this question may be obtained, by considering the use that is likely to be made of the instrument; if the keys which have more than two or three sharps or flats were now, as formerly, but seldom employed, the unequal temperament would be preferable. But as almost all keys are in general use, the equal temperament alone can answer the purpose. To these sentiments I met with a long and almost universal opposition from organ-builders, some of whom asserted that the equal temperament afforded dissonances which were less tolerable to the ear than any of the unequal temperament, which I knew to be greater. This unintelligible objection has given way to the only true criterion, experiment. I have now heard the equal temperament on an organ, and decidedly prefer it to the former method of tuning. I have also had the satisfaction of finding that my opinion is supported by the known practice of Sebastian Bach, who tuned his own instruments according to this system.*

The doctrine of harmonics will also be interesting to the young composer. These are the notes produced by the aliquot parts of the sounding body; whether a harp string, that of

* See Forkel's Life of J. S. Bach.

the violoncello, a voice, a bell, or an organ-pipe. There is, in fact, no such thing as an individual musical sound in nature. What we call a single sound is always attended with less powerful sounds; as the octave, produced by the half of the tube or string; the twelfth, produced by one third; the double octave, produced by one quarter; the seventeenth, or major third, produced by one fifth; &c. &c. An inconceivable number of these combine to produce one note, that of the whole tube or string. When the lower notes of an organ, harp, pianoforte, or violoncello, are sounded singly, an experienced ear will readily distinguish five or six of these harmonics. As the vibrations of a string on the harp or piano-forte subside, the harmonics become more audible. The sound of a voice at a distance has often been mistaken for a chord produced by glee-singers; but, as the voice approached, the harmonics were less audible, and one note only was heard. In bells, the harmonics are heard almost as plainly as the generator. These harmonics may be separated and examined on a violoncello, by pressing the finger lightly on the string while it is bowed upon. They are also the notes produced by blowing through any simple tube, as the horn and trumpet. The harmonics seem to be imitated on an organ by the stops called cornet, sexquialtera, and mixture, which give full chords for every single note that is played ; also by the principal, flute, fifteenth, and twelfth, which furnish one harmonic to each note. When all the stops are out, and only one note sounded, they cause no confusion, though each of these artificial harmonics must be accompanied by its own natural harmonics; but the sounds heard when a full organ is played, if all distinguishable, and equally powerful, would form a most chaotic and unmusical roar. The principal use of the study of harmonics to the young composer is, that they constitute the scales of the trumpet and horn. And though other notes have been added to the horn, by stopping its bole, yet they are inferior as to the quality of their tone to the natural notes. The wild sounds which the wind capriciously elicits from the Eolian harp are the harmonics of its several strings. Some authors of elementary treatises have derived their musical scales from that of the harmonics; others have contended, that the diatonic scales we use are unnatural and improper. According to them, the trumpet, horn, and bugle, as formerly constructed, are the only perfect instruments; however, they have kindly added to their number a Pythagorean harpsichord and an Egyptian guitar. The scale we now admire is dissonant; that which we alter is perfect. We have, in short, every thing to learn over again. Surely, if this be wisdom, we may exclaim, —

Then " ignorance *is* bliss, *'tis* folly to be wise."

Many improvements in the tone of instruments, and in the mechanism of their several parts, may yet be expected from the study of vibrations and sympathetic resonance. The theory of sound, then, though not necessary to the performer, is highly curious, interesting, and in some measure useful to him.

The study of harmony and the rules of composition is of yet greater practical utility. It necessarily induces a knowledge of the clefs,

and a power of reading from score, and of playing thorough bass. A knowledge of the derivation and inversion of concords, the resolution
and preparation of discords, and the construction
of counterpoint in general, will facilitate the
reading of music at first sight, — an object of the
highest importance to any performer ambitious
of being called a musician. An acquaintance
with the various kinds of unessential notes in
melody will improve the extemporaneous performance of them. Rhythm, accent, emphasis,
and the divisions of time, should be well understood, to be properly expressed in the performance. Modulation requires much study, or the
changes of key will resemble the capricious and
unaccountable shifting of scenes in a pantomime.
The treatment of subjects in canon, fugue, and
imitation, must be much studied, to be performed with good effect, or even heard with
due relish. Such are some of the advantages
of the study of composition to the musician in
general; but to young composers a knowledge
of its rules is indispensable. The violation of
these, in the works of a great master, may be

the result sometimes of design, and oftener of unavoidable haste; in those of the juvenile composer, it is always ascribed to ignorance. Some great men, as Dominico Scarlatti, have occasionally endeavoured to dispense with the rules; but it may be questioned whether any thing great, or worthy of imitation, was ever the result. An appeal to the ear is frequently made in defence of the unlawful combination. But to whose ear is it to be made? Surely not to that of the composer, nor to that of the fellow student, even if advanced a little further than himself. The ear of the experienced composer is greatly pained by sounds which affect others only with satisfaction. The rules were either written by, or founded upon the practice of, the greatest masters. When other composers exceed these, in contempt of the rules by which they submitted to be governed, then, and not till then, we may throw them aside as useless incumbrances. *

* See many excellent passages on this subject in Forkel's Life of J. S. Bach.

Enough, it is trusted, has now been said, to induce the lover of music to study the science, which, it will be remembered, is not the proper subject of this work, — that being the improvement of the taste. But permit me to anticipate a few questions which may naturally suggest themselves to the reader ; and, after replying to them, to give a few hints as to the frame of mind which the student should endeavour to assume.

What, it may be asked, is the present state of the public taste in this nation, that it should be thought necessary to interfere with it by a work of this kind ? Is there not already a sufficient number of books on the subject ? Have we not an abundance of critics, connoisseurs, and amateurs ? Is not any one possessed of a musical ear capable of judging what is good or bad for himself ? Is it not for the public that the composer writes ? Whom else should he endeavour to please? — In answer to these questions I assert, then, that the public taste still requires much cultivation, though greatly improved since the commencement of the present century.

Sound principles are more generally adopted as
the basis of critical observations ; good music of
all kinds is more frequently heard and duly appreciated. Yet, taste in perfection is neither universal
nor prevalent. If it is found among the aged and
experienced, it cannot be expected in the young
and untutored, to whom these Lectures are principally addressed : they must not be left to
form their own taste. Small, indeed, are the
advances which an unassisted individual can
make in endeavouring to attain perfection in
any of his powers. What is called human reason is said to be the result, not of the effort and
ability of its possessor, but, of lights mutually
communicated and reflected by the discourse
or writings of many. * The principles of just
criticism must thus be acquired by the musical
student. By criticism, is not here meant (what
it is too often made to signify) the art of censuring in technical terms, and in a learned manner :
but that of separating excellence from defect ;
of admiring, as well as finding fault ; of discri-

* Dr. Beattie's sentiments are here adopted.

minating and comparing the several styles, and
of appreciating their relative value on principles
which are generally true as applied to all the
fine arts. A reference to these principles will
enable us to overturn the absurd and mischievous opinion held by many writers and
the generality of professors of the art, that
music is continually improving from every invention, innovation, and addition, that her suc-
cessive cultivators choose (I had almost said,
happen) to make. Is it possible that novelty
can be the chief requisite, and originality the
only merit, of music alone? The rise and decline of painting, architecture, and sculpture,
have been pointed out, and remedies for their
improvement suggested, without fear of censure.
But our art, it seems, neither has arrived, nor,
as long as another composer shall spring up, can
arrive, at perfection! There have, indeed, never
been wanting those who bitterly and unjustly
inveigh against all innovation. The addition of
a seventh string to the Grecian lyre had nearly
made a martyr of the daring inventor. And
pedants may be found in all ages and climes.

But are we, therefore, not to analyse the merits of a new production? Or must we say that the sublimity and learning of the old Church composers is far exceeded by all their successors?— that it is easy now to write as well as Palestrina did? — that the march in *Mosè in Egitto,* merely because it is in an oratorio, is composed in the true sacred style, and therefore fit for the organ voluntary? But let me not be misunderstood. I am a professed admirer of modern music, and shall endeavour hereafter to do ample justice to its merits. But in writing a course of Lectures for the improvement of musical taste, it is my pride, in imitation of the great lecturer in a sister art*, to call on the student to acknowledge that from them " he has " contracted no narrow habits, no false ideas, " nothing that will lead him to the imitation" or adulation " of any living master who may be " the fashionable darling of the day." If we consult books, we shall find much confident assertion unsupported by sound principles. Every

* Sir Joshua Reynolds, — Sixth Discourse.

style of music has its votaries and champions, both writers and critics, who, like true knights of old, contend that the idol of their admiration shall not only receive the honour due, but be allowed to be unrivalled, pre-eminent, and per- fect. A few can be touched only by the grave solemnity of the church style. The oratorios of Handel are with more the chief source of delight. The modern Italian opera is by many accounted the only school for vocal melody. Some prefer a glee to all other music; the con- cert sinfonia is sufficient for others; while the compositions of the day for the piano-forte is all the music that is known to many. As all styles are thus praised, so all are condemned. Ac- cordingly, we read and hear continually of the dry and pedantic strains of the church, the tedi- ous heaviness of the oratorio, the trifling puerility of the opera, the excruciating dissonance of the German sinfonia, and the affectation and ex- travagance of instrumental music for the cham- ber. How, indeed, can musicians in general acquire the essential requisites of an author or a critic? They generally find that the cultivation

of any one branch of the art precludes all attention to the others.  Mere performers are seldom
better judges of the music they execute, than
actors are of dramatic writings; and, like them,
generally form their judgment from the recep-
tion which their own part meets with from the
public.  I have more than once heard some of
the worst singers of the lowest styles of music
seriously call the song which had just obtained
for them the applause of a tasteless audience,
the finest that was ever written! Performers,
however, both instrumental and vocal, are sometimes possessed of good taste; but it is necessarily confined to the style of music to which
they have been most accustomed.  The choir
singer may be consulted about the merits of an
anthem ; but he is seldom fond of any modern,
and especially instrumental, music.  An Italian
opera-singer will speak correctly of the productions of his own country, but he does not
relish the music of the German school; nor are
foreigners in general judges of ancient music.
And if it is thus with musicians, what can we
expect from the man whose sole qualification for

being a critic is having an ear for music? He may be pleased when hearing it; he may be fond of it; and refreshed by it after fatigue; he may like to be lulled to sleep by it; and the artless murmurs of the Eolian harp will answer the purpose as well as the noblest of scientific productions, which, indeed, would rather keep the true lover of music awake, by arresting and rivetting his attention. This same self-constituted critic, when awake, may find his imagination fired by powerful effects, strong contrasts, and sudden transitions; he may be deeply affected by pathetic expression. But the delicate refinements of taste escape him, and all that is scientific and learned is unregarded or despised; he frequently prefers the worst music, " for" (says the lecturer already quoted*) " it is the lowest style only of " arts, whether of painting, poetry, or music, " that may be said, in the vulgar sense, to be " naturally pleasing. The higher efforts of " these arts, we know by experience, do not

* Sir Joshua Reynolds.

" affect minds wholly uncultivated. This re-
" fined taste is the consequence of education
" and habit." The good composer must not,
therefore, write for the majority of hearers; he
must not be discouraged by the inattention or
censures of the public. Let him look to Sebastian Bach, " who " (says his biographer)
" never worked for the crowd, but always had
" in his mind an ideal perfection without any
" view to approbation. He sung only for him-
" self and the Muses." Were the majority always in the right, why are the Battle of Prague
and Pleyel's Concertante, which they so much
admired, now passed into oblivion to make way
for similar trash? Were the majority always
wrong, we should thus have another rule for
determining our own opinions. But they are
not to be trusted. And when I attend public
concerts, and hear, as is too frequently the case,
the undeserved applause bestowed on some new
trifle, I am tempted to apply to them what Sir
Joshua Reynolds says of the public exhibitions of
paintings,—" Popularity always accompanies the
" lower styles of painting. I mention this, be-

" cause our exhibitions, while they produce such
" admirable effects, by nourishing emulation and
" calling out genius, have also a mischievous
" tendency, by seducing the painter to an am-
" bition of pleasing the mixed multitude of peo-
" ple who resort to them." Certainly, however,
it is the wish of the composer to please, if possible, all hearers — both the discerning few, and
the unpretending multitude. He would, if he
could, acquire both immediate and lasting fame.
He would, if possible, have all men on his side.
He therefore argues with them, and endeavours
to persuade them to adopt his opinions, when he
cannot agree to theirs. These endeavours are
not usually crowned with success. A lasting
reputation is seldom acquired quickly. It is by
a slower process, by the prevailing commend-
ation of a few real judges, that true worth is
finally discovered and rewarded. The opinions
of acknowledged critics accumulate in time, and
are compacted into a mass that irresistibly bears
down before it all the opposition of false taste
and ignorance. Hence, the artist who lives un-
noticed and neglected, often, after death, acquires

immortal fame. Marcello, who was at first too highly extolled, and afterwards as much under-valued, has found his true level among the great classical composers. The Prince of Venosa was hailed as the brightest of the rising luminaries, then suddenly went down, and was no more re-membered. " Giant Handel " was driven by " the Goddess of Dulness " " to the Hibernian " shore," * —but is now placed highest in the temple of Fame. The prevalence of true taste would have altered all these cases, by immedi-ately determining the merits of the candidate. But it is said that the taste of the critic should even equal that of the composer — as in the sister art, " whatever speculative knowledge is ne-" cessary for the artist, is equally and indispens-" ably so to the connoisseur." † Taste cannot be too much or too carefully cultivated.

I now have to offer a few hints on the frame of mind which the student should assume, if he would derive due benefit from the remaining part of the present work.

* Pope. † Sir Joshua Reynolds.

He must place little or no reliance, at first, on his own judgment. He must revere the characters of the classical composers of former ages: they have acquired a celebrity which has outlived and triumphed over the false taste of the times in which they flourished. " He who " begins by presuming on his own taste, has " ended his studies as soon as he has com- " menced them." * Neither let him be dazzled with the sudden blaze of newly-kindled reputation. Experienced critics alone are able to distinguish what is good or bad in new productions; and even they do not find the task easy. He will be sure to meet with those who would recommend their own and other modern works in preference to those of the early masters, " who," say they, " however eminent at the " time they lived, have been long superseded." But " the modern, who recommends himself as " a standard, may justly be suspected as ignorant " of the true end, and unacquainted with the " proper objects, of the art which he professes.

* Sir Joshua Reynolds.

" To follow such a guide will not only retard
" the student, but mislead him. On whom, then,
" shall he rely? or who shall show him the path
" that leads to excellence? The answer is
" obvious. Those great masters who have tra-
" velled the same road with success are the
" most likely to conduct others. The works of
" those who have stood the test of ages have a
" claim to that respect and veneration to which
" no modern can pretend. The duration and
" stability of their fame is sufficient to evince
" that it has not been suspended upon the
" slender thread of fashion and caprice, but
" bound to the heart by every tie of sympathetic
" approbation." *—Who these great masters
were, it may be easy to discover; but the degree
of veneration in which they ought to be held, and
the comparative excellence of their several productions, may not be so obvious to the student.
It is probable that, far from being enraptured,
he would, at first, be disappointed and even dis-
pleased with their works, and tempted to throw

* Sir Joshua Reynolds

them aside as dull, heavy, monotonous, void of feeling, expression, and effect. But to experienced judges they constitute what the remains of antiquity are to painters, architects, and sculptors. Let him, then, " regard them as " perfect and infallible guides; as subjects for " his imitation, not his criticism." *

So great, indeed, ought to be his deference for their superiority, that it has been said, " to " feign an approbation of them would be venial, " as it would probably terminate in sincerity " and true taste." But, as long as sincerity is wanting, a submissive silence is rather recommended.

* Sir Joshua Reynolds.

# CHAP. II.

## ON THE THREE STYLES OF MUSIC—THE SUBLIME, THE BEAUTIFUL, AND THE ORNAMENTAL.

As there are certain principles common to the fine arts, music may be considered in reference to other arts, with a view of improving the taste, by an analogical application, to music, of those principles admitted to be true in respect of the other arts. " To enlarge the boundaries of the " art, as well as to fix its principles, it is neces- " sary that that art and those principles should " be considered in their correspondence with the " principles of other arts, which, like this, ad- " dress themselves primarily and principally to " the imagination." *

On this plan the founder of the British School of Painting, whose just sentiments and forcible

---

* Sir Joshua Reynolds.

language I cannot too often quote, raised an academy, with which, it is allowed, the similar institutions of other nations will not bear a comparison. " It is by the analogy that one art " bears to another, that many things are ascer- " tained, which either were but faintly seen, or, " perhaps, would not have been discovered at " all, if the inventor had not received the first " hints from the practice of a sister art on a " similar occasion. The frequent allusions which " every man who treats of any art is obliged to " make to others, in order to illustrate and con- " firm his principles, sufficiently show their near " connection and inseparable relation. All arts " having the same general end, which is to " please, and addressing themselves to the same " faculties through the medium of the senses, " it follows that their rules and principles must " have as great an affinity as the different mate- " rials, and the different organs or vehicles by " which they pass to the mind, will permit them " to retain." *   " There is, then " (says another

---

* Sir Joshua Reynolds.

elegant author *), " a general harmony and cor-
" respondence in all our sensations, when they
" affect us by means of different senses; and
" these causes (as Mr. Burke † has admirably
" explained) can never be so clearly ascertained
" when we confine our observations to one sense
" only." Music is not, indeed, like painting,
an imitative art, but " applies itself, like archi-
" tecture and poetry, directly to the imagination,
" without the intervention of any kind of imita-
" tion." ‡ There are in music, as in other arts,
certain styles, which are more or less valuable
" in proportion to the mental labour employed
" in their formation." § Music, like painting,
may be divided into three styles — the sublime,
the beautiful, and the ornamental. Sir Joshua
Reynolds does not avowedly adopt this division. He speaks of the sublime and ornamental
only. But that which he calls the sublime evidently includes the beautiful; and that which
he calls the ornamental seems analogous to the

* Uvedale Price on the Picturesque.
† Burke on the Sublime and Beautiful.
‡ Harris's Three Treatises.      § Sir Joshua Reynolds.

picturesque. We cannot peruse the celebrated
work on the Sublime and Beautiful, without admitting that the distinction between them is
there made manifest. " The sublime and beau-
" tiful have been accurately described in an
" essay, the early splendour of which, not even
" the full meridian blaze of its illustrious author
" was able to eclipse." *   " The picturesque has
" a character not less separate and distinct than
" either the sublime or the beautiful; nor less
" independent of the art of painting. The term
" picturesque (as we may judge from its etymo-
" logy) is applied only to objects of sight; and,
" indeed, in so confined a manner as to be sup-
" posed merely to have a reference to the art
" from which it is named : I am well convinced,
" however, that the name and reference only
" are limited and uncertain, and that the quali-
" ties which make objects picturesque are not
" only as distinct as those which make them
" beautiful or sublime, but are equally extended
" to all our sensations, by whatever organs they

* Price on the Picturesque.

" are received; and that music (though it ap-
" pears like a solecism) may be as truly pic-
" turesque according to the general principles of
" picturesqueness, as it may be beautiful or sub-
" lime according to those of beauty or sublimity.
" The English word picturesque naturally draws
" the mind towards pictures; and from that par-
" tial and confined view of the subject, what is,
" in truth, only an illustration of picturesqueness,
" becomes the foundation of it. The words sub-
" lime and beautiful have not the same etymo-
" logical reference to any one visible art, and
" therefore are applied to objects of the other
" senses. Sublime, indeed, in the language
" from which it is taken, means high; and
" therefore, perhaps, in strictness, should relate
" to objects of sight only; yet we no more
" scruple to call one of Handel's Choruses sub-
" lime, than Corelli's Pastorale beautiful. But
" should any person, simply and without quali-
" fying expressions, call a capricious movement
" of Dominico Scarlatti, or Haydn, picturesque,
" he would, with great reason, be laughed at;
" for it is not a term applied to sounds: yet

" such a movement, from its sudden, unex-
" pected, and abrupt transitions, from a certain
" playful wildness of character, and an appear-
" ance of irregularity, is no less analogous to
" similar scenery in nature, than the concerto, or
" the chorus, to what is grand or beautiful to
" the eye." * That this third style may be denominated the ornamental, and that Sir Joshua
Reynolds meant no other, I infer from his using
the expression, " the picturesque or ornamental
" style ; " and this he opposes to that higher walk
of the art which he calls the sublime, and which
includes the beautiful. † An attempt, therefore, will be made in these Lectures to improve
the taste of the student, by enabling him to appreciate the merits of any composition by considering the comparative value of the style
adopted by its author. And if, by this mode of
considering the subject, we find that the art is on
the decline, let us not regret that we have discovered Truth, though she may seem to frown

* Price on the Picturesque.

† I feel much pleasure in finding that Mr. Samuel Wesley,
in his Lectures on Music, has adopted the same division.

on us. Her brightness, which enables us to detect our error, will also help us to recover from it. Let criticism be just, and artists will pay it due respect. Let the higher walks of the art be pointed out, and new productions will soon spring up and adorn them.

Music, then, I repeat, like other arts, may be divided into three styles — the sublime, the beautiful, and the ornamental — which are sometimes distinct, and sometimes combined.

The sublime is founded on principles of vastness and incomprehensibility. The word sublime originally signifies high, lofty, elevated; and this style, accordingly, never descends to any thing small, delicate, light, pretty, playful, or comic. The grandest style in music is therefore the sacred style — that of the church and oratorio — for it is least inclined to levity, where levity is properly inadmissible, and where the words convey the most awful and striking images. Infinity, and, what is next to it, immensity, are among the most efficient causes of this quality; and when we hear innumerable voices and instruments sounding the praises of God in solemn and becoming strains, the most sublime image that can fill the mind seldom fails to present itself — that of the heavenly host described in the Holy Scriptures *, and thus paraphrased by the Poet: —

> ———— " all
> " The multitude of angels, with a shout
> " Loud as from numbers without number, sweet
> " As from blest voices, uttering joy, heaven rung
> " With jubilee, and loud hosannas fill'd
> " The heavenly regions." †

Uniformity is not only compatible with the sublime, but is often the cause of it. That general, equal gloom which is spread over all nature before a storm, is, in the highest degree, sublime. A blaze of light unmixed with shade, on the same principle, tends to the same effect; and, accordingly, Milton has placed light in its most glorious brightness as an inaccessible barrier round the throne of the Almighty.

Simplicity, and its opposite, intricacy, when on a large scale (such an intricacy as, from the number of its parts, becomes incomprehensible), are sublime. Raffael's cartoons are simply sub-

---

* Revel. v. 8—14.; xiv. 1—3.; xv. 2—4.; xix. 1—6.
† Milton's Paradise Lost, book iii. 344.

lime ; Martin's Belshazzar's Feast is a specimen of sublime intricacy. The large portico of the Grecian Parthenon, or the long arcade of the Roman Aqueduct, illustrate simple grandeur* ; and the Gothic cathedral is an example of sublimity resulting from a vast assemblage of parts. In music, the great compass of notes employed in a full orchestra conveys an idea of vastness undefined. A uniform succession of major chords, the most agreeable of all sounds, resembles a blaze of light; while the unintelligible combination of extraneous discords conveys a feeling like that caused by darkness. The clearness of harmony in the madrigal of many voices, or in the full anthem, and the deep science of the organ fugue produce sublimity from seemingly opposite causes ; as also a passage performed by many voices or instruments in

* Several words are here used, for the sake of variety, to denote the sublime style which are not strictly synonymous. Sublimity, elevation, and loftiness are so; but grandeur and magnificence imply something of splendour and agreeable attraction. The military man well knows the difference between the grandeur of a parade and the sublimity of a battle. The choruses of Haydn, Mozart, and Beethoven are frequently magnificent, but seldom sublime.

unisons or octaves, and one in full and florid counterpoint.

Pathetic expression, which will be treated of more fully hereafter, is not confined to any one of the three styles, but is most analogous to the ornamental. In painting or sculpture, sorrow robs the countenance of dignity and beauty, but is conducive to picturesque effect.

Beauty, in all the arts, is the result of softness, smoothness, delicacy, smallness, gentle undulations, symmetry, and the like. When, therefore, in music the melody is vocal and flowing, the measure symmetrical, the harmony simple and intelligible, and the style of the whole soft, delicate, and sweet, it may with as much propriety be called beautiful, as a small, perfect, Grecian temple, or a landscape of Claude Lorraine.

The ornamental style is the result of roughness, playful intricacy, and abrupt variations. In painting, splendid draperies, intricate architecture, gold or silver cups and vases, and all such objects are ornamental; aged heads, old hovels, cottages, or mills, ruined temples or castles, rough animals, peasants at a fair, and the like, are picturesque. In music, eccentric and difficult melody; rapid, broken, and varied rhythm; wild and unexpected modulation, indicate this third style.

The three styles are seldom found distinct. A mixture of the sublime and beautiful, though at first it might seem incompatible with the opposite nature of their characters, is sometimes found. The wisdom of Minerva's countenance, and the majesty of Juno's, did not prevent their being candidates for the prize of beauty, though it was probably the cause of their losing it. In music, when the melody is simple and slow, the harmony full and plain, and the expression chaste and solemn, it will be as difficult to deny the combined existence of the sublime and beautiful as to determine which predominates. Such a combination forms one of the higher walks of our art.

The sublime and ornamental may be combined, as in the landscapes of Reubens and Gaspar. This is closely analogous to the intricate grandeur already described; and it is illustrated in music by those choruses in which the voices are dignified, and the accompaniments varied and playful.

Beauty and ornament are still more frequently blended. " The sublime by its solemnity takes " off from the loveliness of beauty." * The ornamental style " corrects the languor of beauty " and the horror of sublimity, but renders their " impression less forcible. It is the coquetry of " nature; it makes beauty more amusing, more " varied, more playful, but also

" Less winning soft, less amiably mild."

In music, wherever there is flowing and elegant melody, with playful and ingenious accompaniment, this union must be apparent; it forms the leading characteristic of modern music.

The three styles may also be found blended, though rarely without a sensible predominance of that in which the composer excels, or that which is the favourite style of the age in which he lives.

* Price on the Picturesque.

Let us next consider the rank and value of these styles, as the basis on which all the elements of musical criticism may safely be established.

The rank and value of each style are deduced from a consideration of the mental labour employed in their formation, and the mental capacities required for the comprehension and enjoyment of them. From the time of Longinus, at least, who wrote on the subject in the early part of the third century, the invention of whatever is sublime has been esteemed the greatest effort of the human mind. This style, which is emphatically denominated the elevated, the lofty style, may well be called the highest walk of any art. But whether we regard this, with Sir Joshua Reynolds, as including the beautiful, or, with Uvedale Price, divide the whole into three styles, the lowest and least estimated is the ornamental. The well known rebuke from his master of the young Grecian painter, for having decked his Helen with ornaments, because he had not the skill to make her beautiful, is a striking illustration of the inferiority of this style. Difficult as execution, in music or in painting, may appear to the ignorant, it is held in comparative contempt by those who seek for the forms, or the sounds, that can only be produced or enjoyed by the mind. We say, then, with Sir Joshua Reynolds, that the highest walk of the art is the sublime, and the lowest walk of the art is the ornamental. But if, with Burke, we separate the sublime and beautiful into two styles, which shall we prefer? — Surely the sublime, as requiring most mind in the person gratified, and in the author of the gratification. The mental operations required for writing an epic poem, designing a cathedral, painting a storm, or composing a full chorus, must be greater and more extraordinary than those which produce a sonnet, a shrine, a miniature, or an ariette. Why was the lecturer in a sister art so anxious to impress on his pupils the merits of Michael Angelo? Not because he is generally allowed to be the most pleasing of painters; not because he is the last painter, or the favourite of the present day; but because he excelled all others in the sublime style — the pure sublime, not including, in this case, beauty. How many would pass by his productions who would admire, and duly appreciate, the truth of Wilkie, or the minuteness of Ostade! Many turn from the vast, the incomprehensible, the awful, the terrific, to find a milder gratification from that which soothes and tranquillises the mind. A still greater number seek for amusement and delight from the wit and humour of the lowest style. A multitude may be satisfied with, and even prefer, caricatures. A child, a savage, the weakest mind, may be charmed with beauty of any sort, in nature or art — distant views, soft scenery, delicate objects, shells, flowers, minerals, insects, elegant buildings, apartments, or gardens; while the same mind would perceive nothing but terror in the storm, danger in the precipice, desolation in the ruin, poverty in the hovel, and barrenness in the rocky mountain. Some minds may, however, feel what is forcibly striking and grand, while the less obtrusive merits of the pure sublime will not appear to them to have any effect. Pope, Scott, and Byron have charms for all readers. Milton is compre-

hended by few; and that few can remember
how long it was before they could perceive his
excellence. The mind itself must expand before
it can comprehend what is so vast. Admiration, wonder, awe, and even terror are produced
in the mind by the sublime style ; beauty pleases,
soothes, and enamours ; ornament dazzles, de-
lights, amuses, and awakens curiosity. Will it
not, then, be readily granted that the value of
any style, singly, or predominating if combined,
may be ascertained by the nature of its im-
pressions ? To be amused and delighted is a
meaner enjoyment than that of being soothed
and charmed ; while both are less noble to the
mind than feeling itself elevated and expanded.
The humorous incidents of a drama make men
laugh ; the tender and happy parts excite the
smile of approbation : but the tragic scenes
petrify them into silent, serious, breathless attention. The superiority of the tragedy over
the comedy, and of both over the farce, is therefore obvious, though the majority of every audience should deny the statement. Illustrations
out of all the arts might easily be multiplied.

In Grecian architecture the Doric, Ionic, and Corinthian orders are respectively in the sublime, beautiful, and ornamental styles. Show them to the world — the bending acanthus, the rich entablature, and the light proportions of the Corinthian will be instantly preferred by the majority; the chaste elegance and simplicity of the Ionic will charm others; while the massive strength and bold outline of the Doric will be left to the admiration of the remaining minority. Show them, again, the sacred edifices of the twelfth, thirteenth, and following centuries in this kingdom. Some would venerate and admire the ponderous strength of the massive columns and impenetrable walls of the Norman fabrics. More, thinking these heavy and barbarous, would prefer the lighter shafts and aspiring arches of the early pointed style; while the many would be dazzled and delighted with the lofty spires and pinnacles, and the rich tracery in the roofs and windows, of the decorated style; and even more so, perhaps, with the superabundance of ornament in the perpendicular style, which was the sure indication of the decline of the art.

The student has now obtained a rule for discovering and appreciating the value of any piece of music, by observing the effect of its style, or of its predominant style, on real judges. It is sublime if it inspires veneration, beautiful if it pleases, ornamental if it amuses. Whoever, then, were the greatest composers of the sublime style, they are to be regarded as treading in the highest walks of the art; those of the beautiful occupy another inferior stage near the summit; but those of the ornamental are far below. When two of these styles are combined, a union of the sublime and beautiful ranks first, one of the sublime and ornamental next, and one of the beautiful and ornamental last; and when all are combined, the predominance of any one over the others must be regarded with a reference to its own peculiar value. Such a combination of the three as preserves their due subordination, not permitting the beautiful to take precedence of the sublime, or the ornamental of either of the others, deserves the highest praise.

When these styles prevailed, and who these composers were, shall be considered hereafter.

# CHAP. III.

## ON MUSICAL EXPRESSION.

PREVIOUS to the application of the foregoing general principles, and the attempt to show when these styles prevailed, and who were the greatest masters in each, it will be necessary to detain the student on another subject of considerable importance — that of musical expression.

In extolling the descriptive powers of our art, many writers have exceeded the truth, making it capable of what it really cannot achieve. Composers, encouraged by these praises, have become more daring than their predecessors, and have drawn upon themselves the censure not merely of sound musical judges, but of others, ignorant of the art, and only guided by common sense, " who, though deaf to the " charms of music, are not blind to the absur- " dity of musicians." * The union of music

* Dr. Beattie.

with poetry (making vocal music) has been one
fruitful source of these exaggerations. Praise
due to the poetry alone has thus been bestowed
on the music. Let the poetry cease altogether,
or be in an unknown tongue, and then see
whether music can build the walls of a city, or
civilise a savage race. Music has been called
the language of nature; but it is a very imperfect language; it is all adjectives and no sub-
stantives. It may represent certain qualities in
objects, or raise similar affections in the mind to
what these objects raise, but it cannot delineate
the objects themselves. It conveys no imagery;
and cannot even discriminate very accurately
between the affections it does command. It
may speak of something serene, joyous, wild,
tender, grave, melancholy, troubled, agitated,
or pathetic; but without poetry lends her aid
we remain ignorant of what that thing may be.
An argumentative writer tells us, that " the
" fittest subjects for imitation are all such things
" as are characterised by motion and sound.
" Motion may be either slow or swift, even or
" uneven, broken or continuous; sound may be
" either soft or loud, acute or grave. Wherever,

" therefore, any of these species of motion or
" sound may be found in an eminent degree,
" there will be room for musical imitation. The
" glidings, tossings, and murmurings of water,
" the bellowing of a storm, and the confusion of
" a battle, are all capable of being, in some
" degree, imitated in music." And again, he
says, " Music is a modification of sound, and
" rhythm is the time or motion of that sound ;
" musical sounds, therefore, may resemble other
" sounds, and musical motion other motion." *
Let the piece be unaccompanied by words or
title, and the gliding, tossing, bellowing, and
confusion will neither represent water, a storm,
or a battle. Handel has but one and the same
favourite soothing melody to express the murmurings, or perhaps the undulations, of a flowing stream †, the repose of the dead ‡, the beauty
of the queen §, and the softness of spring. ‖  In

* See Harris's Three Treatises.
† Last song and last chorus in Acis and Galatea.
‡ " I know that my Redeemer liveth."— *The Messiah.*
§ " Upon thy right hand did stand the Queen."  " My
heart is inditing."— *Cor. Anth.*
‖ Recit. in Joshua, preceding the song, " Hark ! 'tis the
linnet."

another place, where waves were to be depicted, and the roaring of a giant, but one passage is used. * The poet says well of this composer, that

    " Jove's own thunders follow Mars's drums." †

But the drums are obliged to represent sometimes one and sometimes the other.

The student has learned that awe, complacency, and amusement, are severally caused by the sublime, beautiful, and ornamental styles. ‡ Pain and pleasure are awakened by the use of the minor and major keys, of their appropriate concords and discords, and of the chromatic and diatonic scales. The major key is more agreeable to the ear than the minor, and the diatonic scale and discords than the chromatic. In the diatonic scale there are fewer semitones than in the chromatic, and those further apart. The triads of the major key are the same with the perfect chords formed by any note with its five principal harmonics, and are therefore as much a part of nature as light itself,

* " Wretched Lovers."— *Acis and Galatea.*
† Pope.         ‡ See the preceding Chapter.

or the colours into which it may be refracted. Again, if two notes of the triad are accurately sounded by two voices or instruments, a third sound, belonging to the same triad, is formed in the ear by the coincidence of the vibrations. If C and E are produced in the treble clef, the G below is heard; and if E and G, C below. But the minor key consists partly, and sometimes wholly, of minor triads. Now, the minor triad is not, like the major, a part of nature; nor will two of its sounds generate a third: consequently, it is less agreeable than the major; its minor third seems, like the string which sounds it, to have been relaxed and depressed from the more agreeable and natural major third. While the chromatic scale, abounding in semitones, and its discords containing minor and extreme flat and sharp intervals, approaches nearer to the cries and howlings of men or animals in distress, to the whistling of the wind, and to other confused and indistinct noises, than the diatonic scale. The major key, therefore, when unincumbered with chromatic passages, is a great source of calm satisfaction to the mind; it causes serenity.

By serenity I do not mean indifference, but that tranquil pleasure which ever results from the contemplation of the beautiful style. Some pleasure also accompanies the awe and the pain occasioned by the sublime and the pathetic. Much also depends upon the manner of performing any passage. The same notes which, when rendered by a few soft voices, we pronounce beautiful, acquire somewhat of the sublime by increasing the number of the performers, though still very soft; but if loud, the character is totally changed, and the beautiful disappears. *

Clearness of harmony likewise conduces to serenity; the attention is less fatigued than by what is complicated and unintelligible. Symmetrical rhythm, in moderate time, also conduces to the same effect. By increasing the velocity, joy and delight are kindled. Long accented notes, with short unaccented ones fol-

---

* In Handel's Hallelujah Chorus, the notes to the words, " The kingdoms of this world," when performed soft, are beautiful; but when repeated loud, and with the full band, are sublime.

lowing, convey an idea of firmness and majesty. Very slow notes belong to sublimity, and very rapid ones to ornament. Broken and varied measure is properly used for indecision, as in the song of Jealousy, —

> " Of different themes the veering song was mix'd, —
> " And now it courted Love ; now, raving, call'd on Hate." *

The poignancy of grief in the minor mode is much increased by the agitated rhythm rendering that confused, or mysteriously grand, which in the uniform measure would only have been melancholy.

But if it be demanded whether this is the use always made of the major and minor keys, I am compelled to own that it is not. Many exceptions to the rule may be found in the works of the great masters. Handel has set words to the minor key which seemed to require the major. † The minor key of itself confers an expression of seriousness and dignity, and is frequently on that account adopted by second-rate composers.

* Collins's Ode to the Passions, set to music by Dr. Cooke.
† " How beautiful are the feet !" — " Thou art gone up on high." — " If God be for us."

But Handel was not of this description. He probably adopted the minor key merely for the sake of contrast to the pieces which preceded and followed. Thus the Italian painter considered " *una nevola che passa,*" a sufficient excuse for having thrown a shade over one of his figures that he did not wish to be too prominent. *
Sometimes, also, he adopted the major key for words of a sorrowful cast. Contrast may account for this also ; and, indeed, a succession of pieces in the minor would be yet more fatiguing than in the major key.

The general effect of the oratorio † is improved by these contrasts ; but had the pieces been composed separately they would probably have been differently treated. Observe in the recitative, " For behold, darkness shall cover the earth," and in the air which follows it, how carefully the author has assigned the minor key to the words which speak of darkness, and the major to those of light. The one is set off by

* " Quam multa vident pictores, in umbris, et in eminentia, quæ nos non videmus."— *Cicero.*
† The Messiah.

the other, like the bright gleam of sunshine in a storm, which seems more brilliant than when the whole landscape is illuminated: and this, perhaps, is the reason why the minor key is preferred by many lovers of music — not because it is more agreeable, but that it is a foil to the major key, and makes that more attractive.

In some cases, however, sorrow is not meant by the composer where the words may at first seem to require it. In the song, " He was de-" spised," love to the Saviour, rather than pity for his sufferings, seems intended. And in the movement, " All we like sheep have gone " astray," sorrow for sin was not what the author aimed to excite, but he attempted to depict the thoughtless dispersion and careless wandering of silly sheep, each seeking pleasure its own way. But the practice of disregarding the natural effects produced by the major and minor keys, is by no means peculiar to this author. Instances of it are afforded by the greatest masters of the Italian school, both ancient and modern. Sentiments of the most intense pathos are rendered by music, which we should denominate beautiful. Burke remarks, that the affection produced by the beautiful approaches nearer to melancholy than to joy, according with our bard *, who says, " I ne'er am merry when " I hear sweet music."

But the Italians are justly accused of having less expression and pathos than the Germans. We may instance a song by the elegant Hasse †, " Pallido il sole," the words of which describe the sun pale, the sky lowering, troubles threatening, and death preparing to strike. Yet the key is major, the time moderate, the melody flowing, the expression soft, the harmony clear, the rhythm uniform, and the effect of the whole such as would excite in a hearer unacquainted with its words, nothing short of unmixed delight. " O quam tristis et afflicta!" in the Stabat Mater of Pergolesi, and almost all the opera songs by Sacchini, Sarti, Paisiello, &c. are of this description. This error is not peculiar

* Shakspeare.
† Hasse was a German by birth, but is always considered as an Italian composer, as he wrote in the Italian style.

to our own art. "Guido," says Sir Joshua Reynolds, "from want of choice in adapting " his subject to his ideas and powers, or from " attempting to preserve beauty where it could " not be preserved, has, in this respect, suc- " ceeded very ill. His figures are often engaged " in subjects that required great expression; yet " his Judith and Holofernes, the daughter of " Herodias with John the Baptist's head, the " Andromeda, and some even of the mothers of " the innocents, have little more expression than " his Venus attired by the Graces." In the above passage the real motive is hinted: it was to preserve beauty. The violent passions of grief, and even joy, were destructive of beauty; there are, therefore, but few antique statues which have not tranquil features. And thus the Italian composers, finding themselves unrivalled in the beautiful style, became enamoured of it; and considered it as alone sufficient to constitute perfection. They accordingly threw aside the science which they themselves had invented, abhorring canons, fugues, and learned contriv-

ance, (on which they bestowed the term " sce-
" lerata,") avoiding all but the simplest discords,
and even the minor key itself.

Another imperfection in musical expression is
its incapability of rendering the negative assertion, or the absence of the thing described.   In
setting the words, " When thou hadst overcome
" the sharpness of death," which is the musical
composer to lay hold of?   He cannot convey
an idea of " overcome;" he therefore adapts
the expression " sharpness of death" to appropriate discords.*   Great musicians have been
censured for this.   But would not orators do the
same in their way of pronouncing these words?
" Let the shrill trumpet cease" is a sentence
which absolutely forbids a trumpet to sound
immediately, — which would, indeed, be as
ridiculous, as to begin with a drum when the
poet says, " Not a drum was heard;" but that
the voice in singing these words should use the
scale of the trumpet, would only seem to show

* Handel's Dettingen Te Deum, and that for the Peace of
Utrecht.

that the singer was thinking of what was said. *
In the chorus —

> " No more to Ammon's god and king,
> " Fierce Moloch, shall our cymbals ring,
> " In dismal dance around the furnace blue †," —

the composer was perfectly right in representing
these unhallowed orgies by descriptive music,
notwithstanding the two first words of the
sentence.

Other imperfections in musical expression require to be noticed. " To express," says Dr.
Beattie, " the local elevation of objects by what
" we call high notes, and their depression by
" low or deep notes, has no more propriety than
" any other pun. We call notes high or low
" with respect to their situation in the written
" scale. There would have been no absurdity
" in expressing the highest notes by characters
" placed at the bottom of the scale," or the
reverse, " if custom or accident had so deter-

---

* Last part of " O lovely Peace." — *Judas Macchabæus.*
† First chorus in Jephtha.

" mined. And there is reason to think that
" something like this actually obtained in the
" musical scale of the ancients; at least it is
" probable, that the deepest or gravest sound
" was called summa, and the shrillest or acutest
" ima; which might be owing to the construc-
" tion of their instruments." No person, unacquainted with the fact, could discover that
the symphony in Haydn's Creation, which pre-
cedes the description of the sun-rising, was intended to portray that glorious appearance.
The crescendo, indeed, of the loudness aptly
represents the gradual increase of light. But
the slow progress of the diatonic scale conveys
no idea of ascent or imperceptible motion. In
censuring Handel's attempt to convey the idea
of the sun rising and then standing still at the
command of Joshua, Avison * has made his
ridicule turn upon the composer's endeavouring
to make us hear what could only be seen. But
that does not seem to be the chief objection,
which is rather that the sun is an individual ob-

* On Musical Expression.

ject. Light, created suddenly, or gradually increasing, though only perceptible by the sight,
may be expressed in music *, or, more correctly,
the suddenness or the gradation of some sort of
increase; for light cannot be represented, much
less the sun.

But when composers (however eminent) endeavour to represent, by musical notes, frogs
hopping, arrows flying, a rainbow, a lamp in a
high tower, the depths of the sea, the flight of
an eagle, great whales, crawling worms, tigers
bounding, the paces of the stag and horse, flakes
of snow, forked lightning, a dog running over
the fields, the report of the gun †, and the fall
of the wounded bird, we surely must acknowledge that they have exceeded the true limits of
musical expression.

Another species of imitation in music remains
to be noticed, which is occasionally used with

* See the opening of Haydn's Creation, — " O first created
beam"—(Samson), and the last scene of Weber's Der
Freischutz.

† The report of the gun, as being a sound, is perhaps the
least exceptionable of these imitations, but even that is too
minute for musical expression.

great success : the imitation of sounds, whether those which are unmusical — as thunder, cannon, birds, the roar or murmur of waters, the cries of distress or pain, the whistling of the wind ; — or those which are musical — as the tolling or ringing of bells, or of certain instruments, which, by their tone and scale, and the music peculiar to them, convey the idea of the military, pastoral, or sacred styles. Dr. Beattie, from whom I have already quoted many excellent sentiments, has the following passage on this subject, with which I cannot agree, and which I think liable to be made the foundation of erroneous principles : —

" A flute, a hautboy, or a bagpipe, is better
" adapted to the purposes of rural music than a
" fiddle, an organ, or a harpsichord, because
" more portable, and less liable to injury from
" the weather. Thus an organ, on account of
" its size and loudness, requires to be placed in
" a church, or some large apartment ; thus vio-
" lins and violoncellos, to which any degree of
" damp may prove hurtful, are naturally adapted
" to domestic use ; while drums, trumpets, fifes,
" and French horns, are better suited to the

" service of the field. Hence it happens, that
" particular tones and modes of music acquire
" such a connection with particular places, oc-
" casions, and sentiments, that by hearing the
" former we are put in mind of the latter, so as
" to be affected by them, more or less, according
" to the circumstances. The sound of an organ,
" for example, puts us in mind of a church, and
" of the affections suitable to that place ; military
" music, of military ideas ; flutes and hautboys,
" of the thoughts and images of rural life."
Thus there is between these kinds of music and
the ideas they excite " only an accidental con-
" nection, formed by custom, and founded rather
" on the nature of the instruments than on that
" of the music."

Let us, then, suppose organs and piano-fortes
portable : would they suit the purposes of regu-
lating the step, and inspiring courage in battle ?
Let us imagine violins to be so improved as
not to be affected by the damp : would the line
advance to " the jocund rebeck's sound ?" The
trumpet, cymbal, and drum, are as portable as
the flute and bagpipe. Why, then, do not shep-

herds amuse their shepherdesses and flocks with these deafening instruments? If an organ were reduced in size, and a piano-forte rendered gigantic, might they exchange their situations? It is clear that our author has omitted to make the provision, that the instruments should be calculated to excite devotion, pleasure, or courage; and also, that the music performed on them should always be in the most appropriate style for its purpose. But is our author right in what he has said? Does the sound of the organ always put us in mind of a church? If it did in his lifetime, it too frequently does not so now. It often reminds us of the concert, the drawing-room, the opera, and the play-house, even when heard in a church. The remote sounds of the pealing organ are, indeed, sometimes so blended by echoing along the vaulted roofs of the cathedral and cloister, that they produce the most sublime effects, and we might suppose that the style of the music is that which we call sacred; but a nearer approach will often dissolve the charm. We shall find it is the military, or the pastoral, or the piano-forte style, which

is used for the voluntary. Again, hear a military band on parade playing the soft adagios of
Haydn, Mozart, and Beethoven! Though a
whole host of armed men surround you, not one
military idea is awakened. Hear the same band
in the ball-room, and here also they produce no
military effect. Oboes, flutes, and flageolets are
not properly military instruments, yet they are
added to augment the sound of the band, and,
by playing the same music, increase its effect.
They do not always remind us of pastoral scenes.
On the organ, when judiciously played, we may
distinguish the church and the oratorio styles. On
the piano-forte, though all styles are not equally
calculated to suit its peculiar expression, all may
be distinctly heard, — the sacred, the military,
the pastoral, the concert, the opera, and its own
appropriate style. How then can the style de-
pend upon the instrument alone? The piano-
forte does not imitate the tone of the organ, of
military, or of pastoral instruments. The limited
scales of the trumpet and horn, indeed, are re-
cognised when notes similar to harmonics are
used. But the sacred, the military, and the

pastoral styles are only properly so called when instantly distinguishable from each other, if performed on the piano-forte. Whatever is slow and grave may sound well if performed on an organ; but these qualities do not constitute sacred music, any more than adagios, pastorales, and dances performed by a military band, however well they may sound, constitute military music. I am fully aware that I am opposed to the majority of English organists, and to all foreign musicians, in these sentiments. The practice of organists shows that " The praise " and glory of God" is not so much thought of as their own reputation for execution or invention. They perform on the organ during divine service such pieces as are expressly composed for the piano-forte, concert, or theatre; or pieces which do not differ from them in style. There is, then, between these kinds of music and the ideas they excite more than " an acci- " dental connection;" and it depends as much, at least, on the nature of the music as on that of the instruments. " If the trumpet give an

" uncertain sound, who shall prepare himself for
" the battle?" *

Musical expression is, then, more limited in
its powers than is, perhaps, generally imagined. †
Music cannot, like painting, seize on a particular action, and represent, with minuteness, all
its parts. Like poetry, her imitation is very
inferior to that of painting. Without the aid of
music, poetry is necessarily forced to waste many
of her richest ideas in attempting to raise the
affections,—which, when united to music, she
finds raised already. Without the aid of poetry,
music can awaken the affections by her magic
influence, producing at her will, and that instantly, serenity, complacency, pleasure, delight,
extacy, melancholy, woe, pain, terror, and dis-
traction. She can remind us also of the sacred,
military, and pastoral styles; and when poetry
would speak of the thunder-storm, the battle,
the howl of pain, the warbling of birds, the roar
of the winds or the waves, the breath of the

* 1 Cor. xiv. 8.     † See Harris's Three Treatises.

zephyr, or the murmuring stream, the solemn curfew or the merry peal of bells, music can by her imitations increase, almost infinitely, the enjoyment of the description.

# CHAP. IV.

THE RISE, PROGRESS, AND DECLINE OF THE ART.

WE are next to consider when these styles prevailed; and by viewing the result of this enquiry apart from the names of the great composers we have been accustomed to admire, we shall more readily perceive the degree of credit due to the deductions which follow: we shall be induced to own that criticism, founded on principles common to all the fine arts, is just and free from prejudice.

In all cases where the order of the invention or adoption of the sublime, beautiful, and ornamental styles can be ascertained, we find the sublime is the earliest, and the ornamental the latest; and it is acknowledged that the undue prevalence of the ornamental style is a sure indication of the decline and decay of any art. It was thus in painting, in architecture (both

Roman and Gothic), and in sculpture, which, indeed, hardly admits the presence of this third style in any degree.

As the ancients had painting, and, perhaps, attained to considerable proficiency in it, so they had music also, of which we know but very little. As painting was revived by Cimabue, so our art was revived when scientific music, or that containing harmony, was invented in the eleventh century. The remains of the real music of the ancients * are so scanty, that I can only, on the present occasion, refer the student to two fragments of it, which are in a simple and sublime style, not unlike our sacred music. † National music (or that which has been traditionally preserved in various nations, the authors being generally unknown) is also supposed to be the remains, or at least a close imitation, of the

* By this expression is meant that of the Greeks, Romans, &c.; and it must be carefully distinguished from ancient music, which means that of the sixteenth, seventeenth, and early part of the eighteenth centuries, as opposed to modern music.

† Burney's History, vol. i., or Specimens of Music, by the author, vol. i. p. 14.

music of the ancients. * In this all the three styles existed. The inventor of scientific music † had all these before him ; for, however uncertain the dates of many of the airs may be, there is no question as to the existence of national music anterior to the use of harmony. The Hebrew chants, for instance, noticed by Marcello in his Psalms ‡, are said to be very ancient. They were preserved by the Spanish and German Jews ;—and so strongly resemble the Persian service, (which is also likely to be ancient) that a Hebrew high priest, who heard the latter performed by the suite of the Persian caliph on an embassy at Petersburg, was highly offended, thinking it was done in derision of the Jews. The Chinese § are so remarkably tenacious of old customs, that there can scarcely be a doubt of the high antiquity of their airs, or of those of the East Indies, though we do not indeed suppose the Monk of Arettino was acquainted with these. The Greek ‖ air called Romeka appears

* Specimens, vol. i.        † Guido.
‡ Specimens, vol. i. p. 15.    § Specimens, vol. i. p. 153.
‖ Specimens, vol. i. 145.

to have been modernised in its melody and graces; but not so in its style and measure, which were suited to the dance which has been an annual commemoration, from time immemorial, of the deliverance by Theseus of the young Greeks from the Minotaur in Crete. * The airs of the bards and troubadours were performed all over Europe. The air called the Hymn of Roland was composed before the battle of Hastings, being sung by the Conqueror's army as it advanced: and the Welsh tunes of David the Prophet † and Sweet Richard were deciphered from a Welsh MS. of the eleventh century, and were probably not new when inserted. These, then, I repeat, in their various styles, together with the chants which had existed in the Christian church at least from the fourth century, were equally open to the adoption of the inventor of harmony. In national music, the military, the pastoral, and the dance styles were distinct and appropriate. The difference of

* 1235 years B. C.        † Specimens, vol. i. p. 77, 78.

their character is not caused by age; they will not increase in sublimity by becoming older; they will not become suitable to sacred subjects. The chants adopted by Guido as proper for sacred music, were the Gregorian and the Ambrosian; and these are said to have been derived from the sacred music of the heathen, or perhaps that of the Jews. Thus many of the inventions in architecture, usually ascribed to the Greeks and Romans, are found to have existed in the far more ancient edifices of the Egyptians. This was not, therefore, the invention of the church style, but only of harmony differing from the consecutive 4ths, 5ths, and 8ves, with which their chants had previously been accompanied, and which, if sung softer than the melody, probably produced a similar effect to that of certain stops in the organ, which seem to have had their origin in this species of accompaniment, which was called organum. * These would not alter or destroy the character of the

* See page 8. and 9.; also Specimens, vol. ii. p. 1.

chants themselves, which were sublime. I dwell upon this, because it is a common error to suppose that antiquity alone creates the veneration we feel for church music; and that if its compositions always resemble those composed a century back, this will alone constitute the true sacred style. I should indeed rejoice if all compositions less than a century old were at present excluded from the church service. But looking into futurity, I should tremble for the fate of the sacred style, if modern music in general, or much of that now composed for the church, were to be adopted even a hundred years hence. Few productions of the present day will ever become fit for divine service at all. The rust of antiquity will never constitute sublimity. Having learned the comparative value of the several styles, suppose them to exist when they will, let not the musical student, with some writers, (to whom we are infinitely indebted for every thing but their musical criticisms,) imagine that music is continually improving; that every age is superior to the preceding; and that every new composer is greater than his predecessor:

such a taste, indeed, would be easily acquired *, and of no worth when obtained.

" Ecclesiastical music in the middle ages," says Dr. Burney, " was all derived from the " papal chapel and court of Rome; counter- " point was first cultivated for their use. It " travelled thence to the Hanseatic towns and " the Netherlands, where the affluence which " flowed from successful commerce afforded " encouragement and leisure for its cultivation; " till about the middle of the sixteenth cen- " tury, when, by the general intercourse that " traffic and the new art of printing introduced, " all the improvements in harmony, which had " been made in Italy and the Low Countries, " were communicated to every other part of " Europe, which not only stimulated the natives " to adopt and imitate them, but to improve " and render them more perfect by their own " inventions and refinements." And as long

---

* It resembles the accomodating politics in the old song of the " Vicar of Bray." It is displayed in the daily practice of our young females who, on entering a music shop, simply enquire if any thing new is published.

as the pure sublime style,—the style peculiarly
suited to the church service, — was cherished,
which was only to about the middle of the seventeenth century, we consider the ecclesiastical
style to be in a state worthy of study and imitation,—in a state of perfection. But it has been
gradually, though not imperceptibly, losing its
character of sublimity ever since. Improvements have indeed been made in the contexture
of the score, in the flow of melody, in the accentuation and expression of the words, in the
beauty of the solo, and the delicacy of the accompaniment. But these are not indications
of the sublime. Church music is therefore
on the decline. Sublimity is the highest walk
of our art as of every other. Our art is, therefore, on the decline.

The motett and the madrigal were next invented. Here was sublimity combined with a
considerable, and perhaps equal portion of
beauty. This then formed a lofty, though not
the highest station.

Sublimity alone was not suited to the subject
of the madrigal. The union with beauty was

highly proper. But the madrigal of the seventeenth century has never been equalled; glees have become more refined and highly finished, more varied in style, more replete with discords and modulations, more graceful, and, to the generality of hearers, more pleasing and amusing. But these are not the qualities for which the ancient madrigal is so justly valued.

Then came the cantata, from which the sublime was wholly withdrawn, and a style more appropriate to love ditties was judiciously adopted. The vocal melody became still more beautiful, and the ornamental style was invented; or to speak more correctly, adopted in the accompaniment of the violoncello to the cantata, and in the various instruments for a full band in the opera song. This was a considerable improvement of the lower walks, but not of the highest walk of the art.

In the latter part of the seventeenth century, the separation of the two sisters, music and poetry, again took place, by what is called the invention of instrumental concert music. Yet music without words must have been heard in the symphonies of vocal pieces and in the marches, dances, and other airs of national music, from the remotest periods, in various styles. The first concertos, however inferior they may be as instrumental pieces to more modern productions, contain so much sublimity and beauty, with the ornamental style kept in such due subordination, that we cannot but rank them among the finest works of the art.

The commencement of the eighteenth century furnishes the student with abundance for his contemplation, both from the quantity and quality of its productions. Here he will find the organ fugue (a species of music excelling all others in learned and ingenious combinations,) at its highest state of excellence. The ornamental style had not become too predominant, either in the oratorio or opera. The sublime prevailed in the one, and the beautiful in the other. The oratorios of this period may on this account be said to have arrived at perfection. Whatever improvements may have afterwards been made, were in the instrumental department, not in the vocal, — in the overtures,

or the accompaniments, not in the scientific
contexture of the choruses, or the chaste melody
of the songs, — in the ornamental, not in the sublime or beautiful styles.   In the opera, however,
the expression of the vocal melody was not yet
sufficiently light for secular, and especially
comic subjects, although the sublime and every
thing scientific had been carefully excluded;
the instrumental accompaniment had not acquired its transparency and playfulness of de-
coration; ornament was not sufficiently advanced in vigour to support the feeble steps of
beauty, bereft of her aged companion.   It has,
however, been increasing in strength and importance ever since, and has brought the opera
to the state in which we now find it; more
light, brilliant, and varied than ever, more scientific and more dramatic, though perhaps less
replete with beautiful melody than it has been.
Of the improvement in the instrumental department of the opera, that of concert music
was a natural result.   While science was banished, the overture and concerto remained
uninteresting; but when this was readmitted,

and the sublime occasionally introduced, the modern style of instrumental music became, as such, much superior to what it had been. The ornamental style is necessarily predominant in instrumental music. But in solo concertos for particular instruments, and in piano-forte music in general, it is more obtrusive than in the concert sinfonia, or in the quartett for the chamber.

From the foregoing statement, it appears then, that in modern music the instrumental style is greatly advanced, or perhaps arrived at perfection, but the progress of vocal music is not so apparent. But vocal music is superior to instrumental music, as it includes it as an accompaniment in every thing except glees. Again, sacred music is not improved, secular is. But sacred music is of a higher order than secular. And again, the ornamental style is more cultivated than the beautiful, and the sublime most neglected. Yet the sublime is superior to the beautiful, and both to the ornamental. The art is, therefore, on the decline.

The remedy is obvious, let the young composer study the productions of the sixteenth and seventeenth centuries, in order to acquire the true church style, which should always be sublime and scientific, and contain no modern harmonies or melodies. There will still be room for the exercise of genius, without servile plagiarism. To excel in the madrigal, let him be well versed in the first works of that description. In the oratorio let him use all the styles, preserving their due order so often mentioned. In the opera, let the beauty of the vocal melody be never lost sight of, or obscured by the accompaniment. And in instrumental music, let him endeavour to keep pace with the latest composers. The art will thus be effectually secured from further deterioration and decay.

# CHAP. V.

## THE NAMES OF SOME OF THE MOST DISTINGUISHED COMPOSERS IN VARIOUS STYLES.

I AM now about to introduce the student to the names and works of some of the most eminent only of the great composers in their several styles. I have already shown what frame of mind he ought to assume in order to benefit by the study of them. But I must again caution him, that he will probably be disappointed at first hearing them, especially those to whom he will be first introduced. He will meet with critics and writers who assert that, " whatever does not produce " effect cannot be worthy of our admiration." But the sublime, in every art, though least attractive at first, is most deserving of regard. When Sir Joshua Reynolds first beheld the Cartoons of Raffaelle he felt disappointed, but he afterwards yielded to none in his veneration for their sublimity. For this quality does not strike and surprise, dazzle and amuse, soothe and delight; but it elevates and expands the mind, filling it with awe and wonder, not always suddenly, but in proportion to the length and quantity of study bestowed upon it. The more it is known the more it will be understood, approved, admired, venerated, and, I might almost say, adored.

Let the young musician begin his studies of the church style with chants and psalms. The fragments of chants preserved by Guido should be noticed*, as they contain melodies that have been used as subjects by great masters. The Ambrosian chant, used in the fourth century, is quoted by Bird in his anthem, " Ne " irascaris," — " Be not wroth," — or " Bow " thine ear." The Gregorian chant, used in the seventh century, is quoted by Leo in his Dixit Dominus, in C.† The notes to which Guido proposes a pedale or holding note in the

* Specimens of Music, vol. ii. p. 1.

† Specimens of Music, vol. ii. p. 104. See also a tabula tonorum in Hawkins's History of Music, vol. i. ; and also the Benedictus of Marbeck, in Burney's History of Music, vol. ii.

bass, together with that pedale, form a passage remarkable for its high antiquity; for the pedal note, though called his invention, he must have heard on the bagpipe, and in all national pastoral music : this passage has been used as a half and full close by almost every composer of sacred music, down to the Requiem of Mozart, his last production. A chant composed by Josquin de Prez, in the fifteenth century*, contains two characteristic features of the age in which it was produced : one is the transition from the chord of C to that of B flat, and then back to that of C; the other is concluding with a major chord to the key-note of the minor key of D. The harmonies which Tallis, in the sixteenth century, put to the Litany†, may have been his own; but the chants themselves are older, and are still used for chanting the prayers in most cathedrals. They were applied, in the University of Oxford, with additions by Dr. Aldrich, to the

---

* Specimens of Music, vol. ii. p. 1.

† Boyce's Cathedral Music, vol. i., and Tallis's Latin Litany and old psalm tunes, edited by the author of the present work.

Latin Litany, performed at the University church during Lent. They constitute a perfect specimen of pure sublimity, totally unlike the music of the present day; totally unlike the sounds of singing, harping, piping, marching, and dancing, which their inventors had heard in national music. They are, indeed, what the poet calls

" The voices of the dead, and songs of other years." *

But they are suited to sacred subjects, and remind the hearer of no other style; whereas the voluntaries and psalms of the present day are inappropriate and unbecoming.

The psalms used and composed by the Reformers, (usually called the old hundredth, the old thirty-eighth, &c.,) and those by their immediate successors in this kingdom, (called by the names of places, as London, Windsor, Winchester, &c.,) together with those made in imitation of these pure sacred strains, are alone worthy of study.† And these should be played

* Palestine, a prize poem, by the late Bishop Heber, when an under-graduate.

† See Tallis's Latin Litany and old psalm tunes; also Specimens of Music, vol. ii. pp. 2, 3.

simply, and with such harmonies as are of a suitable style; while all the Magdalen and Foundling hymns, with psalms made out of songs, glees *, and quartetts, in drawling, whining, minuet-like strains, with two or three notes to each syllable, full of modern and chromatic discords, with interludes, symphonies, introductions, shakes, flourishes, cadences, appoggiaturas, and other unseemly displays of the organist's finger or fancy, should be denounced and utterly abolished. " And must we, then, have no new church music?" Yes; but no new style: nothing which recommends itself for its novelty, or reminds us of what we hear at the parade, the concert, and the theatre. Much new music may be produced in the sacred style; though to equal what has already been produced will not be found so easy as may perhaps be imagined.

---

* " I know that my Redeemer liveth;" " Sin not, O King;" " Ah perdona;" " Thou soft flowing Avon;" " Lightly tread;" " Drink to me only with thine eyes:" with Haydn's, Pleyel's, Mozart's, and Beethoven's adagios, have all been made use of as psalm tunes.

If we turn from the consideration of our parochial music to that of the choir service, the splendid collection of Boyce's Cathedral Music instantly claims our attention. Here the student will find the finest chants, services, and anthems that exist, to English words. By studying these, he will acquire that discernment of styles which we press upon him as so necessary. He must not pronounce the music of our countrymen, Tye and Tallis, or of Orlando di Lasso and Palestrina, who flourished in the middle of the sixteenth century, barbarous and antiquated, though we will allow it to be

" Something rich and strange." *

The generality of Tye's music is in a sweet, simple, and clear style; more intelligible than that of Tallis, much of which is in the Dorian mode, or obsolete diatonic minor key of D, without a B flat.† It has been said, that he was not happy in the choice of his subjects; but the

* Tempest.— *Shakspeare.*

† This mode is traditionally preserved by the gallery singers of our country churches. It is also met with in some national tunes, especially Irish.

first part of his anthem, " I will exalt thee, O
" Lord," shews that, in sublimity, harmony, and
pathos, as well as in the choice of his subjects,
he was inferior to no one.* This leads me to
remark, that the student who is unacquainted
with the mysteries of canon, fugue, and imitation,
is unable to appreciate the merits of the ancient
style of music. From the time of Josquin de
Prez, the father of modern harmony, to that of
Handel, no composer was held in high estimation who was deficient in science. Farrant's
style is usually melancholy †; but his anthem,
" Lord, for thy tender mercy's sake," is in the
major key, — serene, clear, and as beautiful as
so simple a melody could be. The movement,
" Deposuit potentes," from a Magnificat by
Palestrina ‡, possesses great freedom of motion
in the melody. Dean Aldrich (whose valuable
collection of anthems, masses, madrigals, and

---

* Specimens of Music, vol. ii. p 4.; and Boyce's Cathedral Music, vol. ii.

† See Gloria Patri, Specimens of Music, vol. ii. p. 5., and
Anthem.

‡ Specimens of Music, vol. ii. p. 6.

cantatas, English and foreign, of the sixteenth and seventeenth centuries, is left to the Christ Church Library, Oxford,) adapted many of the finest portions of the works of Palestrina, Bird, Carissimi, and others, to English words, as anthems for our church. Such is the full anthem, " We have heard with our ears, O Lord *," by Palestrina, which is in a rich, dignified, and sober style, the subjects natural, and the management of them skilful. †

The madrigal at the latter part of the sixteenth century having arrived at perfection, its beautiful style insinuated itself gradually into church music. To the names of great composers already mentioned, we may now add those of Monteverde, Gironimo Converso, Luca Marenzio, and Emilio dal Cavaliero; and of our own nation, Bird, Morley, Dowland, Weelkes, Wilbye, and Este. To an inexperienced ear, the music of this period seems all alike, whether sacred or secular ; accordingly, the madrigal by

* Specimens of Music, vol. ii. p. 6.

† See also " O, give thanks," and " Out of the deep," Aldrich, both from Palestrina. Boyce's Cathedral Music, vol. ii.

Luca Marenzio, " Dissi a l'amata mia lucida
" stella *," has been made into an anthem,
though in itself one of the finest specimens of
the true madrigal style. The difference will be
more perceptible by comparing it with the anthem
already mentioned, " Bow thine ear," by Bird *,
a music master of Queen Elizabeth. This is
in five real parts, and the first subject, a frag-
ment of the Ambrosian chant, is treated with
consummate skill. The second subject, to the
words, " Let thine anger cease from us," is
homogenous, yet sufficiently distinct from the
former; and the first part ends with the major
third in a minor key, called the tierce de Pi-
cardie. The words, " Sion, thy Sion is wasted
and brought low," are set to a most tender yet
solemn passage of plain counterpoint, containing
a transition from the triad of the key-note to one
a whole tone lower, the effect of which is sublime,
and marks its age. This part, though not specified
to be slower and softer than the rest, is usually
sung so ; and I think it extremely probable that
this method of performing it has come down to

us by tradition from the time it was composed. So Allegri's celebrated mass for Good Friday, a composition which will not, upon the whole, bear a comparison with this, produces an awful effect when sung by voices alone, as has always been the case, and with soft, loud, and other effects not marked in the score. For it is a great, though common error, to suppose that the music of this age was void of expression and effect in the performance. At the words, " Jerusalem is wasted quite," and at those of " Desolate and void," appropriate subjects are proposed and sustained; the latter reminding us slightly of the first subject, or Ambrosian chant, with which the anthem commenced, and with which it also now concludes, the bass in particular repeating it several times in an emphatic manner, in the same key, near the close. Upon the whole I know no other such specimen of what is called fine writing, and of the pure, sublime, and sacred style. Till the student can convince himself that any other composition is more excellent in these respects, he may regard it with undivided admiration. This great man produced fine music in many styles. His other anthems in Boyce's Collection are excellent. His canon, three in one, on the fourth and eighth below, " Non nobis Domine *," notwithstanding some little objections to which it is justly liable, and which he might easily have avoided, is an universal favourite, and the most pleasing, perhaps, of all the canons that ever were written. His madrigal, " My mind to me a kingdom is †," possesses great richness of harmony, and its subjects are well treated. His variations to an old national tune called " The Carman's " Whistle ‡ " are ingenious and scientific, and, though difficult, are the easiest of many composed for Queen Elizabeth by several eminent musicians of the day, and preserved in her virginal book : these evince that considerable execution was acquired on keyed instruments at a period when the ornamental style is not usually conceived to have existed.

At the close of the sixteenth century, recitative was invented by Jacobo Peri, in setting an opera

* Specimens of Music, vol. ii. p. 11.
† Specimens of Music, Appendix, p. 154.    ‡ Ibid. p. 155.

called Dafnè. Songs in national music must have been used from the remotest ages. But, in order, perhaps, to be truly dramatic, composers did not adopt them at this period into their operas, and the only melody resembling an air in the above opera is a sinfonia for three flutes in the genuine pastoral style.*

Oratorios differed from operas at this time as motetts differed from madrigals, principally in the words which were sacred instead of secular. But the chorus, " Fata festa al signore," from the oratorio called " Di anima e di corpore," by Emilio dal Cavaliero, printed at Rome, 1600, (the earliest that is preserved,) will show that the true church style was clearly distinguished from the pastoral at this period.

Orlando Gibbons flourished in the seventeenth century, and the study of his works cannot be too strongly recommended. For pleasing subjects, skill in the management of them, — for the artful contexture of the score and the flow of melody in each part, — he is pre-eminent. Im-

* Specimens of Music, vol. ii. p. 12.      † Ibid.

provement in the accentuation and expression of the words may be perceived in his admirable, short, full anthem, " Almighty and everlasting God." *
Writing in a score consisting of many parts was, at this time, much in favour, and became the test of a composer's abilities. It is, accordingly, required by the statutes of the university of Oxford, that the exercise for the degree of bachelor in music shall be in five voice parts, and that for a doctor's in six or eight, besides instrumental accompaniments ; and though this task may be accomplished without taste, invention, or originality, it cannot without previous study, application, and experience. Gibbons's anthems, " O clap your hands † " and " Hosanna to the Son of David," are in a score of many parts, and well written. His service in F is the best we have ; the Sanctus is very fine. The Gloria Patri to the Nunc Dimittis ‡ is a canon, two in one, possessing as much elegance

* Specimens of Music, vol. ii. p. 14.

† Boyce's Cathedral Music, vol. ii.; and Specimens of Music, vol. ii. p. 12.

‡ Specimens of Music, vol. ii. p. 17.; and Boyce's Cathedral Music, vol. i.

and freedom in the melody of its parts as if not shackled by the rigid laws of this species of composition. In the madrigal style this author was also eminent. "Oh, that the learned poets" is a masterly production. But his little glee for five voices, " The Silver Swan *," is inferior to no English composition of the kind.

Carissimi was alike successful, whether writing for the church, oratorio, or chamber. He was the father of that more polished and beautiful vocal melody which has characterised Italian music to the present day. Of his twenty-two cantatas in the Christ Church library at Oxford, there is not one but offers something that is still novel and elegant. The aria " Sin' ch'avro " spirto e vita † " is nearly as beautiful as those composed a hundred years after, and possesses scarcely a feature by which its age could be suspected. The movement, "Amanti che dite‡," which concludes his serenata " I naviganti," for three voices, shows his skill in the management of his subjects, and the originality, pathos, and

* Specimens of Music, vol. ii. p. 18.
† Ibid. p. 19.         ‡ Ibid. 20.

expression of his style. The motett for the festival of St. Peter and St. Paul, " Hodie Simon " Petrus *," contains many peculiarities of manner, in which he was followed by Bassani, and other good composers, — one of these is the constant repetition of each new passage, a fourth or fifth above or below, having its origin, probably, in canons. The modulations and transitions are excellent, particularly a change from major to minor, near the beginning. The contrast between passages resembling recitative, and those which have air, and between those that are slow and quick, serene and pathetic, is deserving of study. Carissimi was one of the numerous composers of whose inventions and combinations Handel availed himself. In most cases he merely took ideas, and greatly improved them ; but when he introduced the passages entire and unaltered, it must be considered as a quotation of a well known classical author, and not as plagiarism, which results from poverty of invention, and with the hope of escaping

* Specimens of Music, vol. ii. p. 21.

detection. " When Raffaelle borrowed from
" Masaccio, he improved upon his model; but
" when he copied from the antique (as for the
" sacrifice at Lystra), he took the whole, much
" as it stands in the original."—" His known
" wealth was so great, that he might borrow
" where he pleased without loss of credit. The
" work from which he borrowed was public, so
" that, if he had considered it a disgraceful
" theft, he was sure to be detected. But he was
" well satisfied that his character for invention
" would be little affected by such a discovery;
" nor is it, except in the opinion of those who
" are ignorant of the manner in which great
" works are built."* Carissimi's chorus, " Plo-
" rate filiæ Israel," from his oratorio of Jephtha†,
remarkable for its double discords and bold
transitions, is quoted by Handel in his choruses, " Hear, Jacob's God," Samson, and
" Father of Mercies," Joshua. From the same
oratorio, the short chorus, " Et ululantes
" filii Ammon‡," may be seen at the end of

* Sir Joshua Reynolds's Lectures.
† Specimens of Music, vol. ii. p. 21.     ‡ Ibid. p. 22.

the chorus " With thunder arm'd," Samson.
" Et clangebant tubæ" is imitated in the symphony of " We come in bright array," Judas
Macchabæus. The lamentation of Jephtha over
his daughter, " Heu mihi, filia mea," is em-
bodied in the recitative " He chose a mournful
" muse," Alexander's Feast. And from another
work of Carissimi Handel has taken his subject,
" If there was any virtue," in the Funeral Anthem; and which had been previously adapted to
the words, " For he hath delivered my soul from
" death," by Aldrich. The approbation of such
a master as Handel, and the slightness of the
alterations made in the passages adopted, convey
stronger praise on Carissimi than I could bestow.
Of three movements, with which one of his
masses in the Christ Church collection concludes, " Deum de Deo," and " Et resurrexit*,"
are on ground basses nearly similar; but in the
latter the bass changes its key in an unusual
manner. The last movement contains passages
of canon and imitation, and terminates with a

---

* Specimens of Music, vol. ii. p. 24.

fugue on a double subject, full of ingenuity and solemn effect.

Alessandro Scarlatti of Naples, in the latter part of the seventeenth century, wrote in various styles, but excelled particularly in cantatas, of which he was at once the most voluminous and ingenious composer.* " Fortunati miei martiri†" is replete with elegance and originality, and might well be taken for an opera song of Handel, who has, indeed, adopted some of its cadences, and frequently made this great master his model. The character of the melody, particularly that of the accompaniment, is quite unlike all the music we have hitherto noticed. Instrumental music for keyed instruments had, as we have seen, been made long before; but this composer seems to have been one of the first to apply the ornamental style to vocal chamber music, and to the opera full band; his

* Faustina, a great singer, the wife of Hasse, remarked to Dr. Burney, that the warm eulogy passed on Durante by Rousseau in his Musical Dictionary would have been more duly bestowed on Scarlatti, his master, whom she considered as the most original of all composers.

† Specimens of Music, vol. ii. p. 26.

son, Dominico Scarlatti, carrying the same style to the greatest possible excess in his harpsichord lessons. The bass part of the air " Perche geme, O tortorella *," both in the symphonies, and where it accompanies the voice, consists of a most eccentric melody, to which the student would find it difficult to put a pleasing treble; but the air is of an opposite character, plaintive, natural, and beautiful. In " Voglio amar †" the passages are spirited and expressive; they are, indeed, all repeated; which produces a tiresome effect, when they are all of the same length, so that the mind can anticipate what follows; but this is not the case in the present instance. " Non dar piu pene, " O cara ‡," is a beautiful melody, and its bass forms a continuous accompaniment, like those of his contemporary of Rome, Corelli. In " Che piu brami §," the minor key expresses grief, and the major an indignant complaint; in the conclusion, the minor sixth and third upon the fourth note of the key occurs: this is a very

* Specimens of Music, vol. ii. p. 26.      † Ibid. p. 28.
    ‡ Ibid.                    § Ibid, p. 29.

pathetic chord, so much used at Naples as to have acquired the name of the Neapolitan sixth, and has been thought to be derived from the ancient Greek music. The skill of this great master in composing opera songs, with orchestral accompaniments, may be perceived by consulting the second volume of Specimens.* His masque of " Venere, Adone, ed Amore," in the Christ Church collection, has an overture in the style of Corelli, whose concertos he perhaps had heard. Dr. Burney mentions six concertos by Scarlatti, for the church, printed in England, early in the eighteenth century, and speaks in high terms of their fugues, harmony, and modulation.†

It is unnecessary to notice all the numerous composers who followed in this style; compared with Scarlatti, they are defective in ingenuity, variety, and playfulness of accompaniment. Stradella, the celebrated singer, composed in a

* Specimens of Music, vol. ii. p. 32—41.

† I have never been fortunate enough to see this work, nor have I met with any one who had; and I shall be extremely happy if this notice of it should again bring it to light. Much may be expected from such a master.

stiff, artificial, and pedantic manner, resembling that of our countryman Travers. "Chi dirà che nel veleno," * is the most spirited, and, upon the whole, the finest specimen I have seen of Stradella's works.

Let the student recollect, that though the beautiful and the ornamental were thus advancing rapidly towards perfection, the sublime was necessarily banished; and it was a lower walk of the art that was improving, while the highest was beginning to be neglected. The state of our English church music of the latter half of the seventeenth century will con-firm this position. The names of Rogers, Blow, Child, and Croft, do honour to our country, not only for their science, but for the improvements they so evidently made in melody and expression, rendering their works more pleasing, and more fit for common use, than those sublimer ones which had preceded them. Anthems, especially solo and verse anthems, were properly made more beautiful than full anthems and services.

* Specimens of Music, vol. ii. p. 63.

Anthems of this kind were continually improving till the time of Green, who lived still later; but though many respectable composers have followed down to the present time, who, with various degrees of success, have increased the quantity of useful church music, I should recommend the student to make a model of no one after Green or Boyce; and if he would excel in the sublime, let him principally study Bird and Gibbons. The "Gloria Patri" of Croft, in A, in the second volume of Specimens *, has a peculiar clearness of harmony, purity of melody, and force of modulation. For grandeur of effect, it is perhaps the best we possess. Durante, the pupil of Alessandro Scarlatti, produced Masses of which the choruses were in the style already invented, while the songs were more original and modern. In this plan he was followed by his pupils Pergolesi, Terradellas, Piccini, Jomelli, Sacchini, Traetta, Guglielmi, and Paisiello. And I cannot but wish that there never had been

* Page 96.

choral composers who have not endeavoured, or
who have failed in their endeavours, to cultivate
the sublime style in their choruses. Durante
was one of the first to conclude his fugues
abruptly, either by plain counterpoint, or by a
cadence of a more modern cast than the rest of
the movement. If a fugue be a barbarous invention, unworthy of an ingenious composer, let
it be omitted altogether. But I should rather
say, it is one of the most interesting of all kinds
of movement, resembling the discourse of a great
orator, who, having chosen his theme, states it
clearly; examines it in all its bearings; views
it through all its changes and varieties of aspect;
and, in conclusion, by recapitulating the whole,
stamps his argument strongly on the mind.
If, then, such a musical composition ends
abruptly, it must be like the oration of one who
fails to bring his argument to a conclusion, or
flies from the question, and changes the subject
of his harangue. The invariable result of such
a practice must be disappointment in the hearers.
The vocal duets of Durante, constructed on subjects of his master Scarlatti, surpassed all others

for learned processes, chromatic melodies, and extraneous modulation. They were long recommended by singing-masters as excellent practice for pupils; and certainly whoever could preserve a correct intonation in singing these crudities, would be likely to find most other melodies easy. But the practice of difficulties will never induce feeling and expression. " Dormino l'aure estive " * is the clearest and most interesting of all his compositions that I have heard. Durante applied the inventions of Alessandro Scarlatti, intended for the cantata and secular subjects, to sacred words; and in thus confounding the styles he has had but too many followers.

Arcangelo Corelli was the reputed inventor of instrumental music. Compared with his cotemporaries Alessandro Scarlatti and Henry Purcell, who also produced instrumental pieces, Corelli was inferior in genius, science, and variety. He was also a mannerist: manner is only upheld by its novelty; it ceases to charm

* Specimens of Music, vol. ii. p. 66.

when it is no longer new. His continuous
basses, however, have never been entirely laid
aside, but are occasionally heard in the most
modern music. A concerto of Corelli is still
an interesting piece in a concert, especially
in one consisting of sacred music, and performed in a church; but more than one would
fatigue and cloy the attention, because they
are so much alike. In this respect they were
justly compared, by an excellent musical
critic *, to the landscapes of Claude Lorraine. Each was a perfect whole considered
by itself, but in a collection of them there
was but little variety. Corelli also produced
trios for two violins and a bass, and solos for
the violin, which are still reckoned the best
practice for the young performer on that instrument. † Matthew Locke's music to Macbeth is
still so frequently performed at our theatres and
the concert of ancient music, as to need no

* The late Mr. Malchair, leader of the music-room orchestra at Oxford for about forty years, and also drawing-
master.

† Specimens of Music, vol. ii. p. 68—77.

praise from me. Kieser and Colonna were also celebrated at this period. Clarke and Goodwin were English composers for the church, of a more pleasing but less dignified style than their predecessors. I merely mention Lotti, and Gasparini, and hasten to consider the works of our immortal Purcell.

Who has equalled him in the pathetic? Who has such forcible expression? His facility of writing in the most learned and intricate styles is extraordinary. The passages which appear laboured and pedantic in others, seem natural and easy to him. He is sometimes artless and simple; but his works abound with harmonies of the most complex and difficult construction, even when he does not seem conscious of manifesting any uncommon powers. But where the nature of the subject and of the words demand a display of his gigantic strength, he amazes us, and surpasses all his rivals. His style is quite original: whatever flows from his pen is peculiar to himself; no one had anticipated it — few succeeded in imitating it. He had his followers; but they soon ceased, unable to controul and direct such vast machinery. His music is often " rich and strange," * but never vulgar. It has the unfortunate property of making all other music (excepting pure old church music and Bach's Organ Fugues) appear common and insipid. I scarcely know a recitative that I held in higher estimation than that which forms the opening of the third Act of Handel's Oratorio of Saul. Yet I remember comparing it with Purcell's Saul and the Witch of Endor †, and the effect was as if I had mistaken the pieces. Purcell produced both vocal and instrumental music, for the church, oratorio, stage, and chamber; thus resting his merit both on his individual and collected talents. He was sublime, beautiful, and ornamental; and the latter styles were not too predominant. But had he no defects? Yes, — such as Milton had. The mind that at all comprehends him is kept continually on the stretch. It is a strong sight that can

* Tempest.
† A part of it may be seen in the Specimens of Music, vol. ii. p. 89.

take in his designs; he is often incomprehensible; the summit of the mountain is hid
in clouds. His sublimity is seldom of the pure
and simple kind, but vast and complicated.
His melodies are often fascinating and bewitch-
ing, yet not eminently vocal and beautiful. His
passages for the trumpet are difficult, and not
productive of good effect. The subjects of his
fugues in his sonatas * are abruptly quitted, and
exchanged for others. The long divisions for
the voice in his songs are ungraceful and
tedious; and the frequent repetitions of mono-
syllables, and of small portions of a sentence,
are absurd and offensive. These are spots in
the sun. But they are spots, not objects for
imitation and praise. His vocal music should
never be attempted by foreigners; and it suc-
ceeds so little in general even with natives
that those who have heard it sung by Norris,
Bartleman, and Mrs. Bates, can scarcely bear to
witness the attempt. I refer to the works already mentioned †, and to a new edition of his

* Ibid. pp. 84. 86.
† Boyce's Cathedral Music and Specimens of Music, vol. ii.

sacred music by Mr. Novello, for examples of
his productions for the church. All his anthems are fine, particularly " I was glad ; "
his services also. But the canons to the
Gloria Patri do not sufficiently exemplify the
art of concealing art. His sonatas are more
scientific and varied, but less pleasing and
artless than those of Corelli. All his dramatic
music is excellent : that to the Tempest is
remarkably clear and simple. When the infant
state of instrumental music is considered, the
original Overture to King Arthur must appear
an extraordinary effort of genius. * It is a
martial symphony, on subjects so simple in themselves, that no one could have compacted them
as our author has done. The music before the
play is from one of his " Wellcom Songs," and
is a chaconne †, or ground bass of eight bars, on
which it was the fashion to compose variations.
Corelli has it in his sonatas. Locke makes
the witches in Macbeth use it. Handel em-

* Specimens of Music, vol. ii. p. 90.
† Specimens of Music, vol. ii. p. 91.

ploys it more than once in his harpsichord lessons, and in one place with sixty-three variations. Those by Purcell are deserving of the deepest study and attention. The chorus, "Brave " souls to be renown'd in story, * " though written with much science and labour, is clear and intelligible. The second movement, which speaks of the death of these heroes, is highly pathetic, and seems evidently imitated by Handel at the conclusion of his chorus in the Messiah, " All we like sheep," to the words, " And the " Lord hath laid on him the iniquity of us all." In the last movement of this chorus are admirably depicted the festive dance and song expected by the Druidical faith to be enjoyed in Woden's Hall. His three mad songs in the Orpheus Britannicus, " From rosy bowers," " Let the " dreadful engines," and " From silent shades," are the finest of their kind, and worthy of the highest praise and admiration. But we cannot speak of many of his songs and rounds on account of the words. Have we no Hercules of

* Specimens of Music, vol ii. p. 94.

the present day to cleanse away this Augean filth, and to render the study and performance of all his vocal music a safe and delightful employment? We ought not to be unacquainted with any work of this man, who was not only the greatest master of his time, but the most extraordinary genius that this nation ever produced.

The Abbate Steffani was admired and copied by Handel. The duet in his " Qui diligit " Mariam " * may be seen imitated in the chorus, " Music, spread thy voice around," Solomon. Caldara excelled in the higher walks of the art. Green and Marcello have already been mentioned.† Galliard's hymn of Adam and Eve, and the Te Deum of Baron D'Astorga have immortalised their names.

Leonardo Leo was considered by Handel the greatest composer of his day. He particularly excelled in writing on a canto fermo. His choruses are not however equal to Handel's. The subjects are not treated with much

---

* Specimens of Music, vol. ii. p. 99. † Ibid. pp. 29. 123.

skill; and the perpetual use of one of them, started by Josquin de Prez in the fifteenth century, and used by Handel in his Amen at the conclusion of the Messiah, though a very fine one, is almost unaccountable. In his Solfeggi it occurs in almost every page, unconnected with the rest of the movement. I lament, that want of attention to the management of subjects in choral compositions is manifest in more than one Italian composer of this period. The endeavours to make a modern termination to a fugue instead of the ancient recapitulation of subjects on a pedale bass, are very unsuccessful. The termination of two fugues in Leo's "Dixit Dominus" in C.* are of this nature, and interrupt the general satisfaction which the rest inspires.

Pergolesi died at the age of thirty-three. Had he lived to attain more experience, we should not probably have had to complain that his fugues discover some puerilities; that he was somewhat of a mannerist; and that

* Specimens of Music, vol. ii. pp. 106. 109.

he was less successful in the sublime than in the beautiful and ornamental styles. His invention was great. Handel has occasionally adopted some of his thoughts, and in Haydn's " Stabat Mater," that great and original master has made Pergolesi his model. Pergolesi's " Sta-" bat Mater" and " Salve Regina" have been published and duly appreciated in England. The vocal melody of his airs is not only always beautiful, but frequently more so than any that has ever been produced. The false expression of the words can only be excused on a principle already noticed\*; discords and minor triads are less pleasing to the ear than concords; pain distorts the countenance; to preserve beauty, the musical composer, like the sculptor or the painter, chooses to sacrifice expression. But there are other instances of inattention to expression not so easily accounted for. In most of the Italian oratorio composers of this period, we find the words " Kyrie Eleeson," " Lord, " have mercy upon us," which, in the early

\* Page 54.

chants of the church, were set to notes the most sublime, solemn, and appropriate, adapted to rapid fugues, which, detached from the words, would express ardour, fury, agitation, any thing rather than pious contrition and prayer.* The chorus, " Gloria in excelsis †," is brilliant and sonorous, well known and deservedly admired. In his secular productions, Pergolesi was still more eminent. His serious opera of Olimpiade is full of grace and elegance, and La Serva Padrona was the first intermezzo of the comic kind that attracted universal admiration. The cantata, with instrumental accompaniments, was carried to perfection by this great composer. The air, " Euridice e dove sei,"‡ for the grace and expression of its melody, and for the skilful imitations and rich harmony pervading a score of five real parts, stands unrivalled, and shows that he was worthy of the high reputation he acquired, which procured for him the title of " Il divino Pergolesi."

* Specimens of Music, vol. ii. p. 110.
† Ibid. p. 114.        ‡ Ibid. p. 116.

The life of John Sebastian Bach, written by Forkel, has been already noticed* as translated into English, and containing just sentiments and sound principles of criticism, while the lives of Haydn, Mozart, and Rossini, better known, I fear, and more accordant with the sentiments of the generality of lovers of music, are calculated to counteract all I am endeavouring to establish. As I am about to consider the works of Bach, let me be permitted, in the first place, to speak more at length of these sound principles of musical criticism, which will be met with in the perusal of his life. The necessity of an intimacy with all music, ancient and modern, to form the taste; the superiority of ancient church music, particularly choral fugues; the unrivalled sweetness of Italian vocal melody; the advance and improvement still made in instrumental music; the comparative value of these several styles; and the conclusion that the art is on the decline, because the higher walks are neglected: these are the

* Page 17.

positions which I would establish. In his pre-
face, Forkel says, " It is certain, that if the art
" is to remain an art, and not to be degraded
" into a mere idle amusement, more use must
" be made of classical works than has been done
" for some time past." All that this writer has
remarked, respecting the impropriety of introducing the ornamental style of the clavichord
into the church, should be particularly noticed
by young organists and composers. He mentions Bach, and his son, William Freidemann, as
elegant performers on the clavichord. " But "
(says he) " when they came to the organ, no
" trace of the clavichord was to be perceived : the
" melody, the harmony, the motion" (rhythm),
" all was different; all was adapted to the
" nature of the instrument, and its destination.
" When I heard William Freidemann on the
" clavichord, all was delicate, elegant, agree-
" able, and pretty. When I heard him on the
" organ, I was seized with reverential awe. All
" was grand and solemn. The same was the
" case with Sebastian Bach in a higher degree."
With the sentiments of the next quotation I

most heartily subscribe my concurrence:—" The
" destination of the organ" (to support church
singing, and to prepare and maintain devout
feelings by preludes and voluntaries,) " requires
" that the composition and connection of the
" tones be effected in a different manner from
" what is practised out of the church: the
" common, the trite, can never become solemn,
" can never excite a sublime feeling; it must,
" therefore, in every respect, be banished from
" the organ. And who was ever more strict
" in this point than Sebastian Bach? Even in
" his secular compositions he disdained every
" thing common; but in his compositions for
" the organ he kept himself far more distant
" from it; so that here he does not appear like a
" man, but as a true disembodied spirit, who
" soars above every thing mortal." I always
suspected, and many years ago hinted in my
Lectures, that the fugues of this author, since
published by Messrs. Wesley and Horn, were
not intended for the organ. It appears, by his
life, that they were composed for the clavichord,
which the author tuned according to the equal

temperament, of which also I always declared my preference.*   In the year 1801, I dedicated an entire lecture to the subject of design in composition, the connection of subject, and of key, with other particulars, which I have continued to recommend to all my pupils in harmony, in defiance of being thought pedantic.   In correcting the compositions of his pupils, Bach always insisted, " not only on the highest degree of " purity" (correctness, freedom from the violation of rules,) " in the harmony itself, but " also on the natural connection and flow of " melody in the parts ; " for although no one passage should be in all respects like another, yet every variety should agree with, and appear to be the almost necessary result of, what preceded it.   Modern music would be considerably improved by the attention of our young composers to the following observation : — " Every " period of ten years has some forms or turns " of melody peculiar to itself; and which, ge- " nerally, grow out of fashion before it expires.

* Page 7.

" A composer, who thinks to have his works
" descend to posterity, must take care to avoid
" them." He will meet with a thousand ad-
visers, who would exhort him to seize them
with avidity, and make them his own. Some
parts of the following passage might well be
supposed to flow from the pen of Sir Joshua
Reynolds : — " The greatest genius " (says Forkel), " with the most unconquerable propensity
" to an art, is, in its original nature, nothing
" more than a disposition, or a fruitful soil,
" upon which an art can never properly thrive,
" except it be cultivated with indefatigable
" pains. Industry, from which all art and
" science is properly derived, is one of the first
" and most indispensable conditions. It not
" only enables genius to make itself master
" of the mechanical resources of the art, but
" gradually excites judgment and reflection
" to take part in all that it produces. The
" ease with which genius makes itself master
" of many of the mechanical parts relating
" to musical composition, and its own satis-
" faction, as well as that of others, with the

" first essays, which are far too early looked
" upon as successful, frequently seduce it to
" pass over the first principles of the art, to
" venture on difficulties before it is fully master
" of what is easy; or to fly before its wings are
" grown. If such a genius is not led back at
" this period by good advice and instruction, or
" by the attentive study of classic works, in
" order to recover what it has neglected, it will
" uselessly lavish its best strength, and never
" attain an elevated rank in art: for it is certain
" that great progress can never be made, nor
" the highest possible perfection attained, if the
" first principles are neglected; and that people
" never learn to overcome great difficulties, if
" they have not overcome what is more easy.
" And, lastly, that no one can ever become
" great by his own experience only, but must
" profit by the knowledge and experience of
" others." Speaking of public applause, he
justly observes, "Most artists are led astray by it;
" especially if it is given them too early; that is,
" before they have acquired sufficient reflection
" and self-knowledge: the public requires every

" thing to be human; and the true artist ought
" properly to make every thing divine. How,
" then, should the applause of the multitude
" and true art exist together? *  The artist may
" form the taste of the public," — but not the
public that of the artist.

I have not wandered so far from my subject
by these quotations as I may seem to have done.
It was on these principles that Bach became
the Michael Angelo of our art, as Handel
was our Raffaelle. Raffaelle is generally acknowledged to be the greatest of painters,
on account of his excellence in many styles;
although Sir Joshua Reynolds seemed inclined
to prefer Michael Angelo, on account of his
sublimity.  Handel may thus be preferred, because his vocal music and choruses are superior to Bach's, and for the vast variety of
his excellence; while for science and elevation
of style (particularly in the composition of
fugues), for the power of abstracting the mind
from all surrounding objects, and so relieving it

* See pages 20 and 21.

from care and sorrow itself, Bach is unrivalled. The study of all his works is therefore earnestly recommended. The four volumes already mentioned as published in this country should be in daily practice. The fugue in the major key of E * is perhaps the best of the whole. The fourth in C sharp minor, on three subjects, if the temperament of the organ be equal, or if it be transposed into C minor with three flats, is suitable to the church. Six of his fugues are printed in three lines, with pedals for the organ. One from another work is on a subject resembling the beginning of a psalm tune called St. Ann's. All these are extremely fine, evincing a depth of learning and skill in the science to which no other master ever attained.

Charles Henry Graun excelled in all the styles, both separate and combined. The Te Deum, the Death of our Saviour, and some masses, are all that I have seen of his works, and they evince his greatness. Many of these

* Specimens of Music, vol. iii. p. 1.

may be seen in the selection of sacred music by the Rev. C. J. Latrobe. *

George Frederic Handel may be called the idol of the English school, as the last-mentioned composer was of the Berlin : both died in 1759. Handel's worth is estimated upon the principles already so often detailed. He did not exceed all others in any one particular style. Bird, Palestrina, Gibbons, and Bach, were more sublime. Purcell was more extraordinary and pathetic. Pergolesi and Hasse were more beautiful. Dominico Scarlatti, and all modern composers, are more ornamental. But if that composer is to be declared the greatest, who, like Raffaelle in the sister art, was great in all styles, not, however, suffering the beautiful or the ornamental to predominate, about six candidates only present themselves : Purcell, Leo, Pergolesi, Graun, Hasse, and Handel. If the last-mentioned is the greatest of these, we know the result. To form his style, he quoted and

* Specimens of Music, vol. ii. pp. 127, 128.

imitated all the great masters. * He wrote in every style. He did not, indeed, compose what we properly call church music, in which the voices are accompanied only by the organ; but all those choruses in which the accompaniments are merely replicates, moving in unisons and octaves to the voice parts, may be considered as such. He could scarcely equal, and was therefore not expected to exceed, the great masters of this style. His organ fugues are on natural and interesting subjects, admirably treated, and are inferior only to those of Bach. In chamber music his instrumental trios were superior to those of Corelli. They show, however, that he was aiming at a higher walk of the art; for they contain subjects better adapted for overtures and full choruses, to which he afterwards applied them. His solos for the flute and violin, on the plan of Corelli, are pleasing. His vocal

---

* Handel quoted or copied the works of Josquin de Prez, Palestrina, Turini, Carissimi, Calvisius, Uria, Corelli, Alessandro and Dominico Scarlatti, Sebastian Bach, Purcell, Locke, Caldara, Colonna, Clari, Cesti, Kerl, Habermann, Muffat, Kuhnau, Telemann, Graun, Mondeville, Porta, Pergolesi, Vinci, Astorga, Bononcini, Hasse, &c.

duets, though inferior as to vocal melody to the great Italian composers of his day, are superior in variety of style and boldness of effect. His Suite de Pieces pour le Clavecin, on the plan of Mattheson's, are greatly superior in harmony and science both to them and to the more ornamental productions of Dominico Scarlatti, Alberti, and Paradies. The fugues are particularly good. As a composer of concert music, our author was excelled by none of his day. His organ concertos are not the best of his works, though some of the movements are admirable. His twelve grand concertos for stringed instruments only, and those called the oboe concertos, from their containing concertante passages for the oboe and fagotti, are all interesting, and some of them (as the first, fifth, and eleventh of the former, and the second and fourth of the latter,) are immortal productions. Handel's operas, though less known than his oratorios, contain fewer vulgar and boisterous melodies, and more that are in the true Italian style of the day. The same difference, however, existed between the German and Italian schools, as has been so

remarkable ever since. The vocal melodies of
Hasse, Porpora, Veracini, Pescetti, and Bononcini, were more light and beautiful; but for
force, variety, design, invention, harmony, and
instrumental effect, Handel was greatly superior to all his contemporaries.

His overtures were, like the other similar
productions of the day, on the plan of Lulli,
consisting of an introduction and fugue. He
seems one of the first who introduced wind
instruments into the score, and to have
added a final air of the minuet kind, as to
Berenice, Faramondo, Ariadne, and to the oratorio overtures of Saul, Samson, Alexander's
Feast, and Hercules, which are all beautiful.
His marches also seem never to have been surpassed. His recitatives, both with and without
accompaniments, in his operas and oratorios, are
full of just expression: take those for example
in Samson. His airs, duets, trios, and other
vocal pieces, form the great mass of our vocal
music to English words. And when we consider he was a foreigner, it is extraordinary
that he should have succeeded so wonderfully

in the expression of the language, and should only be eclipsed by our native Purcell. But for oratorio choruses his pre-eminence is still more indisputable. For learning, pathos, and sublimity, what choruses equal them? Hear them worthily rendered, as at Westminster Abbey, with a band of 1000 performers, and the most magnificent choruses of modern authors appear, by comparison, light and puerile.* This has been owned even by foreigners unaccustomed to ancient music, on occasions where there were only half as many in the orchestra as at the performances just alluded to.†

Hear him in the simple sublime style of the sixteenth century. As in the following pieces: — " Their bodies are buried in peace, but their " name liveth evermore," Funeral anthem. " Since by man came death," Messiah. " He " is my God," Israel in Egypt.‡ Or in those

* Page 34. note.

† As the music at the commemoration of Handel in 1784, and in the following years, was the finest ever composed, so the performances were the best ever heard; all other concerts, when these are remembered, seem, by comparison mean and trifling.

‡ Specimens of Music, vol. ii. p. 144.

original efforts which he occasionally makes in the most sublime style, yet unlike all that is heard elsewhere, as the passages in the Dettingen Te Deum, " The heavens and all the powers therein ; " and " The Father, of an infinite Ma- " jesty ;" and the opening of " Worthy is the " Lamb," in the Messiah. All his choruses on the subjects of mourning show his skill in the pathetic ; and those in which he employs the full orchestra, his powers in the expression of intricate grandeur, or a mixture of sublimity in the voice parts, with ornament in the ac- companiments. The sublime and beautiful are equally united in " Then round about the starry " throne," Samson. Sometimes all the three styles are equally prominent, as in " The listening " crowd," Alexander's Feast * ; and sometimes the sublime is properly withdrawn, as in the Nightingale chorus, " May no rash intruder," Solomon. † Pure beauty, without the grand or the ornamental, may be found in " Questo è il " cielo," the first chorus in Alcina. Can Pur-

* Specimens of Music, vol. ii. p. 146.   † Ibid. p. 148.

cell, Leo, Pergolesi, Graun, and Hasse, individually, (I might say, altogether,) furnish such versatility of talent, with such consummate judgment and science, as our author? If not, the conclusion is inevitable; — the greatest of all musical composers is Handel.

Having guided the steps of the student to this lofty summit, let him contemplate the prospect and enjoy the enlargement of his views. He must surely now regard as beneath him the scenery which he once most admired, but which is, by comparison, so limited and humble. He may not, perhaps, choose to dwell on this eminence, and in every direction he may easily descend; but it is hoped he will frequently revisit these higher walks, which raise him far above all earthly and common sounds, and in their stead give him sublime and sacred strains, which

> " Dissolve " him " into ecstasies,
> " And bring all heaven before" his " eyes." *

Giovanni Adolfo Hasse, pupil of Alessandro Scarlatti, excelled in all styles, but the beautiful

* Milton.

often predominated. For sweet and flowing melody, powerful, varied expression, a rich and clear harmony, and natural and interesting modulation, Hasse is inferior to no composer. He was free from manner, never tedious, never noisy, never barren; but in his most trivial productions there is always something elegant and interesting. His opera songs are frequently excellent; as, " Non a ragione ingrato," " Ombra " cara," and " Cara ti lascio." His " Salve Re-" gina" is a pleasing work. The specimens in Latrobe's collection are good, especially a chorus from his opera of Agostino, " Inspira, O Deus." But the finest of his works seems to be his oratorio of I Pellegrini. *

Tartini, celebrated for his important discoveries in the theory of sound †, composed for the violin; and the subjects, modulations, and style of his solos, are extremely ingenious and pleasing. ‡

---

* See the overture, a quintett, and the last chorus. Specimens of Music, vol. ii. pp. 129—137. The air ascribed to Vinci, vol. iii. p. 8., has been since discovered to be by Hasse, also that in p. 10.

† Stillingfleet's Principles and Powers of Harmony.

‡ Specimens of Music, vol. iii. p. 2.

Francisco Geminiani was, like Tartini, only an
instrumental composer, and his concertos have no
wind instruments. He was a very correct writer,
and distributed his melodies equally to all the
parts. His first concerto, op. 2., is very pathetic
and dignified. The sixth, op. 3., is in the sublime style of the church, and very fit for the
organ.* The Siciliana of the second, op. 2., is
very beautiful; and the first of op. 3. is brilliant,
sportive, and fanciful; and still often heard in
our concerts. He was inferior to Corelli in
clearness and simplicity, and to Handel in boldness and variety. The second of the concertos
by Ricciotti, a name said to have been assumed
by an Italian nobleman, is remarkable for the
rich effects produced by seven obbligati parts. †
Those by Avison and Martini were less sublime
and beautiful than those of their predecessors,
though occasionally very good.

Dominico, the son of Alessandro Scarlatti,
finding it impossible to supersede the productions for the harpsichord of his rival Handel,

* Specimens of Music, vol. iii. p. 12.　　† Ibid. p. 16.

struck out that more ornamental, humorous, or witty style, which gave birth to most of the eccentricities and novelties of modern piano-forte music. To insure originality, he set the rules of composition (which he never violated in his vocal productions) at defiance. In his works we accordingly find but little sublimity and less beauty, but all is calculated to amuse and surprise, to create a smile if not a laugh * ; they are free, however, from one great fault of the modern school, they are not too long. Soler † was one of the numerous imitators of Dominico Scarlatti, some of whom assumed his name. The eighteenth and nineteenth of his sonatas are excellent. It is remarkable that some of them, and of those ascribed to Dominico Scarlatti, have notes for what we call the additional keys. Another style of harpsichord music was invented by Alberti, and continued by Zipoli, Wagenseil, and Crispi‡ ; the characteristics of

---

* Specimens of Music, vol. i. p. 6.
† His lessons were published in this kingdom.
‡ Specimens of Music, vol. iii. p. 32—37.

which were merely a childish simplicity and
great sweetness of melody. Paradies * endeavoured with success to blend the styles of
Dominico Scarlatti and Alberti. Sublimity is
not to be found in his works, but he is elegant
and amusing. He has unfortunately preserved
a striking defect of both the styles he copied, —
the repetition of every passage as soon as it is
heard. There cannot be too much repetition in
any piece of music, but it should be so managed
as not to be anticipated by the hearer. This
defect is not found either in the ancient or
modern great masters. It is conceded to the
admirers of the above masters, that the peculiar
character of the instrument for which they wrote
was elicited and displayed by their compositions,
and that in this respect they improved harpsichord music. But when all sublimity and
science were banished from every style, we
may conclude that music had arrived at her
lowest ebb. Nicolo Jomelli studied under Leo
and Durante, and totally changed the style of

* Specimens of Music, vol. iii. p. 22.

vocal music in Germany, by introducing all the modern inventions into the oratorio. His Betulia Liberata is highly spoken of. In his requiem, the first movement * is a fine representation of repose; and the expression of the words " lux " perpetua," by a long holding note in the alto, is very happy. The fugues are well written, but terminate abruptly †, not with the subjects, but a totally different style of passage. His oratorio of the Passione appears to me inferior to the requiem. The recitatives want expression and dignity; the modulation, however, of the accompanied recitatives is good. The airs are light; the divisions, the closes, the accompaniments are trifling. The rosalia, or repetition of a passage one note higher, frequently occurs. The overture commences with a short adagio, which has been a model to succeeding composers, down even to the Zauberflote of Mozart, which reminds us of it. The allegro is elegant, but theatrical, undignified, and unfit for a sacred subject. The finale, however, is yet more unbe-

* Specimens of Music, vol. iii. p. 26.    † Ibid. p. 29. 31.

coming, resembling the last movements of the overtures by J. C. Bach and Abel, which had no excellence of any kind but their novelty. Lapse of time has conferred no venerable quality on this species of movement, nor ever can. The chorus " Quanto costa" commences with an excellent subject, which has been imitated by Sarti and others; but it is scarcely heard in all the parts before the movement is abruptly concluded. The act concludes with a half close to the word " pensaci." The chorus which concludes the whole * contains more science than those already mentioned, and the expression of the words, " Ne' dubbi passi dell'umana vita," rendered by syncopated notes, and those " a " confidar nella celesti aita," by uniform and accented ones, is very happy. The Italians of this period, as has been already remarked, called the introduction of any thing scientific into opera music " scelerata," — wicked. The epithet would have been better applied to the introduction of any thing trifling or vulgar into sacred

* Specimens of Music, vol. iii. p. 30.

music; such as the practice of introducing modern instrumental music into our church service, already noticed. * The Chaconne of Jomelli (a pas seul for an opera dancer) I have heard performed as a voluntary, and seen set to the responses in the communion service.

Charles Philip Emanuel Bach could write in a style worthy even of John Sebastian †, but is more remarkable for being the father of modern music, to whom Haydn acknowledged himself more indebted than to any other composer. A fantasia by this author will exemplify this fact. ‡ The last movement of Haydn's first sinfonia, composed for Salomon's Concert, is copied from it.

Galuppi, a most voluminous composer, excelled in the comic opera style, which was elegant, light, and trifling. His oratorio of Jephtha contains some beautiful movements,

* Pages 61. 63. 71. 100. 114, 115.

† See Clementi's Practical Harmony, vol. i. p. 110., and Latrobe's Selection.

‡ Specimens of Music, vol. iii. p. 38.

particularly a duet, " Verro mi lascia." His Miserere is pleasing, but void of sublime and sacred expression.

John Christian Bach introduced the clarionet into our opera orchestra. His style was clear and sonorous, like that of Jomelli. His accompaniments were more conspicuous for richness of harmony than his voice parts for sweet and polished melody. He studied contrast, opposing the loud with soft passages, as a principle, and carefully marking them in writing. Such contrasts and other refinements as the double dot, and the various degrees of staccato and legato were formerly acquired in the rehearsals from the directions of the composer only, and not written down. The modern style of instrumental full music, which first originated in the accompaniments and symphonies of Italian songs and overtures, proceeded to improve slowly among composers whose names are now scarcely remembered, as Richter, Kamerlocher, the two Stamitz, and others. The concertos and concert overtures of this period were nearly the same as opera overtures, consisting of an allegro, a slow movement, and a finale. One in three flats by Bach is remarkable for the clear simplicity of its allegro *, and the excellent instrumental effects of its andante. La Clemenza di Scipione is one of his best operas. The overture, though not equal to those which have been produced since, was a manifest improvement on the style of Jomelli. The air " Confusa abbandonata" was heard with satisfaction in our public concerts within these few years. The chorus " Provi " l'Ibero infido " is very appropriate to the stage—not void of ingenuity and choral effect, yet less scientific than the oratorio chorus.

Bach was opposed by Sacchini, whose style of opera music was extremely elegant; and the latter was followed by Sarti, Bertoni, and numerous others, the school closing with Paisiello, Cimarosa, Meyer, and Paer; and a new one being formed by Rossini, which is more gay in its comic parts, more ornamental in its vocal melody, more brilliant in its accompaniments,

* Specimens of Music, vol. iii. pp. 42—47.

and more striking in its effects. But as this forms the style of the present day, I return to the period of which we were speaking.

Charles Frederic Abel established, together with Bach, a concert at the Festino rooms, Hanover Square, which very much furthered the improvement of instrumental music in this country. Concertante pieces, in which Cramer *, Fischer, Bach, and Cervetto, performed on their respective instruments, the violin, the oboe, the piano-forte, and the violoncello, were produced by Bach for the occasion. Abel's overtures were chiefly remarkable for their slow movements. Those of Gossec and Vanhall had more spirit and variety ; but at length the sinfonias of Haydn came, and eclipsed all others. One of the first was long called the Festino Overture, from having been first heard at the above mentioned rooms.

Gluck's opera overtures were perhaps the first of the present school ; and it may well be questioned, whether a grander than that to

* Father of J. B. and F. Cramer.

his Ifigenie in Aulide was ever produced. *
Piccini was a rival of Gluck's at Paris. But
however superior the melody of his voice parts
for sweetness and elegance might be, there
seems no question whether his overtures could
compare with Gluck's. It has been an acknowledged practice with many composers to
write the overture after the rest of the piece
was finished; and this is discovered by its containing quotations from parts which follow, —
parts which were not likely to have been copied
from the overture. Thus Handel's overture to
Deborah contains two of the choruses. Cherubini's to Anacreon contains allusions to almost every scene in the piece; and Gluck's
overture to Ifigenie commences with the notes
for the priest, with which the drama opens.
Martini's overture to Henry the Fourth employs the military instruments with good effect;
and the air " Charmante Gabrielle " makes an
excellent contrast as a slow movement. Gre-
try's overtures were remarkable for brilliance

* Specimens of Music, vol. iii. p. 48.

and gaiety. Those of Cherubini, Mozart, and Beethoven, now so well known, are more scientific, and demonstrate the improvement of instrumental full music.

Vanhall's overtures (more properly sinfonias) have been noticed * : he conduced much also to the elegance of sonatas for the harpsichord †; or, rather, as it was specified on the title-page, for the harpsichord or pianoforte — the latter instrument not entirely superseding the former in this country till the commencement of the present century, although invented in the former half of the eighteenth century in Germany. The inventor of the grand piano-forte was Schröder of Dresden; the maker Silvermann. The invention was also claimed by Castofali of Florence. The Forthier, or square piano-forte, was invented by Freiderici, an organ-builder at Gera, in Saxony, about the year 1758.

Vanhall's quartetts have considerable merit for richness and sweetness ; Schröeter's sonatas

* Page 137. † Specimens of Music, vol. iii. p. 74.

and concertos for the piano-forte abounded with polished melody; Schobert's with rich harmony and considerable spirit *; Boccherini's with science and pathos. His quintetts are admirably written, and are still deserving of study. † Clementi may be called the father of piano-forte music; for he many years since introduced all the beauty of Italian melody into pieces calculated, by their ornamental varieties, to elicit the powers of the instrument, and display the taste as well as the execution of the performer.

Haydn, whom we have already mentioned ‡, formed another school of instrumental music, which continues to the present day. Of his vocal sacred productions his Stabat Mater is the best. The first chorus is learned, ingenious, and dignified; the songs for a bass voice are extremely fine, and the accompaniments throughout the piece delicate and fanciful, particularly that to the chorus " Quis est

* Specimens of Music, pp. 76—81.     † Ibid. p. 82.
‡ Page 137.

" homo." The extraneous modulations and passages in counterpoint are, in all his works, admirable: his fugues are, on simple subjects, not treated with much skill, the interest often declining instead of increasing, and the terminations being abrupt, or in a modern style. His oratorio of the Creation contains the same merits and the same defects. The Chaos is awful, but contains passages that want dignity. The recitatives are in a common style. The principal excellence lies in the accompaniments; but the use of the full orchestra, including trumpets and drums for five or six movements in succession, is fatiguing to the ear, and diminishes their effect. The opening of the third act, " In rosy mantle," with the duet and chorus which follow, " By thee with bliss," is however a happy mixture of all styles in their due place and proportion; a most masterly production, and worthy of study. His oratorio of the Seasons, and his choral masses, have generally the same characteristics as above. Compared with the productions of the former half of the eighteenth century, they are deficient in sublimity and science. His opera of Orfèo contains some fine airs; and indeed the style of his vocal music seems much more adapted for the opera than the oratorio. His detached songs are admirable. His cantatas, " Ah, come " il core," with orchestral accompaniments, and " Arianna in Naxo," with only the piano-forte, have great merit, particularly the latter, which scarcely knows a rival. His canzonets are the best ever composed, particularly the first set. But it is chiefly as an instrumental composer that we acknowledge the unrivalled powers of Haydn. His sonatas for the piano-forte, like Handel's Suite de Pièces pour le Clavecin, seem to have been written, not to display the powers of the instrument, or the execution of the performer, but to gratify the ear and the mind of the hearer; and if studied with this object kept in view, they will appear preeminent and perfect. His quartetts are allowed to be unrivalled. And the number of sonatas and quartetts he produced is astonishing. His Passione Stromentale is not in the church style. The addition of voice parts to it by Michael

Haydn was no improvement; but in its original state, considered as an instrumental piece, it is full of science, pathos, and gravity. The finale, intended to depict an earthquake, is deficient in dignity of style. Haydn's sinfonias *, for number, variety, novelty, brilliancy, and gaiety of style, surpass all others. It was this gaiety which was objected to when his compositions first appeared. But it is this alone which renders them more pleasing and amusing than the equally scientific productions of his pupils Mozart and Beethoven †, both for the piano-forte and the orchestra. Pleyel and Kozeluch were also pupils of Haydn. ‡ The quartetts of the former and the piano-forte sonatas of the latter were once much used. Pleyel's music was light and pretty; Kozeluch's full of propriety, taste, and elegance; but both were inferior to Haydn, Mozart, and Beethoven, in originality, genius, and science. Upon the whole we must

* See one of them, Specimens of Music, vol. iii. p. 146.

† Specimens of Music, vol. iii. p. 125—137., and Appendix, p. 158.

‡ Ibid. 86—109.

consider Haydn as the greatest of all instrumental composers.

The piano-forte sonatas of Mozart are not written with the sole view of displaying the powers of the instrument, but frequently contain effects which resemble those of the orchestra, and even of particular instruments, as the horns. But a more delightful use cannot be made of the piano-forte than to remind us of the full music which we have heard in the orchestra.* His sonatas, with obbligato accompaniments, are sometimes called trios and quartetts. They are among the best of his works. His violin quartetts and quintetts abound with fine writing; but there is a sombre cast which renders them less amusing than Haydn's. The subjects in particular are less beautiful and attractive. The same remarks will apply to the

* A connoisseur, while Mozart was playing, thought to shew his judgment by remarking how much better that passage would sound in an orchestra ; Mozart, however, shut the book, offended, saying, " I wrote it for the piano-forte !" The same thing might have occurred to Handel and Haydn, who wrote for the gratification of the mind, and not for the display of the instrument, or the execution of the performer.

sinfonias of Mozart, which seem to have been produced by a more laborious effort than those of his master. As a vocal composer, however, Mozart was unrivalled by any of his cotemporaries. His operas are decidedly superior to those of Glück, Bach, Haydn, or Winter, in vocal melody, and to all the productions of the Sacchini and Rossini schools in science and harmony, particularly in the overtures, though inferior to the latter in the comic and buffo parts. He is more easily comprehended, and more regular in his phraseology and rhythm, than Weber. The serious opera was better suited to his style than the comic. As a choral composer, the generality of his masses are too light and similar to his opera music for sacred subjects. But his last production, the Requiem, is finer than Haydn's Stabat Mater, and in a more sacred style than his Creation and Seasons; and we, therefore, consider Mozart as the greatest of all modern composers.

The piano-forte music of Beethoven, when it does not abound with difficulties of execution, is original and masterly, frequently sub-lime. His sinfonias are wonderful productions. That he has ever diregarded the rules of composition is to be regretted, as there does not seem to have been the least good obtained by it in any one instance. The opera overtures of Beethoven, Cherubini, and Weber, are extremely fine and deserving of study. The operas of Weber and Spohr and the sinfonias of Mendelssohn are full of science and good writing. The solo concerto for every kind of instrument has been greatly improved in harmony and instrumental effects. Those for the violin by Viotti deserve particular notice.

English vocal music is not, upon the whole, an object for study; but our glee composers have been numerous and respectable. Cooke, Stafford Smith, Webbe, Calcott, and many of their followers, will be immortal.

One other style of music remains to be noticed, which succeeded that for the piano-forte by Haydn, Kozeluch, Clementi, and Mozart. Dussek's sonatas were more difficult and less beautiful than these. But there was a brilliancy and an ornament adapted to the instrument, which laid the foundation of a new school, especially for the piano-forte concerto, to which we consider Steibelt, Woelfl, Cramer, Moscheles, and even Hummel to belong, though the latter is also a follower of Mozart.

Here then I conclude the subject of this chapter, having unintentionally omitted the names of some former great masters, and also, contrary to my original design, mentioned some of those now living. If, however, the characters here given be correct, the result of the statement will be found in the conclusion of the foregoing chapter *, which I need not repeat; if incorrect, let them be altered and amended, but still on the immutable principles already laid down, on which basis alone true criticism can be supported.

# CHAP. VI.

## ON THE PRESENT STATE OF THE PUBLIC TASTE OF THIS NATION.

When church music had become neglected, and oratorio composers were no more, the opera not arrived at perfection, and the concert sinfonia, if performed, not listened to; when playing on the harpsichord or piano-forte had become an indispensable part of polite education, yet the fashionable composers for these instruments were Nicolai, Sterkel, Staes, Eichner, and others, whose names are nearly forgotten : at such a period we may fix the lowest decline of taste in this nation; and this was within about thirty years of the close of the eighteenth century. At this time the musical world of connoisseurs were divided into two opponent parties, the admirers of the ancient and modern styles; the one despising the trifling melodies of the opera, and the other the barbarous and mechanical structure of the fugue. The introduction of Boccherini's quintetts, of Haydn's quartetts, and Clementi's sonatas, into our chambers, and particularly of Haydn's sinfonias into our concerts, in all which beauty of melody and scientific harmony were apparent, stamped a value on modern music which many of the admirers of the ancient school were disposed to acknowledge; but when Mozart became the universal favourite, the long-desired reconciliation between these parties was easy. The lovers of the ancient madrigals, anthems, and choruses, could not but appreciate the vocal full pieces in the operas of this great composer. Science could no longer be held in ridicule; if admired in one author, it must be equally so in another. That which Mozart praised and imitated, could not be despised by his own devotees. Of Handel he always spoke with reverence. He adapted his music to German words, expressly that his countrymen might perform and value it; and this he often did without making any alteration, though at other times he consulted the taste of the hearers, and endeavoured to render it more palatable by what they would call improvements.

Salomon's concerts were chiefly intended for the cultivation of modern and instrumental music, in this nation the German sinfonia being its chief attraction* ; while the vocal concerts encouraged the performance of choruses of the old school, and especially of English ancient madrigals and modern glees, for which our countrymen are so deservedly esteemed pre-eminent. Both these concerts failed eventually; probably owing to the limited nature of their views. The admirers of ancient music, in this nation, were not at this period diminished; though, on the Continent, from the custom of performing the works of the last favourite composer exclusively, till another succeeded him, they had died away. Thus the two parties remained opposed. The attack was vigorous, the defence determined : the performances at Westminster Ab-

---

* Haydn composed twelve sinfonias for them. Mozart was to have done the same, but died just before he was expected here.

bey *, and the concert of ancient music, enabled the old school to hold out, till the pacification already mentioned, effected by the introduction of Mozart's music, took place.

A veneration for ancient music being thus established, or rather revived, on the Continent, foreigners can no longer persuade us to despise a style frequently quoted by Mozart, Beethoven, and Rossini. Differences of opinion concerning the merits of the ancient and modern, of the German and Italian schools, and of various individual composers, still, indeed, continue to exist; but they are constantly diminishing, and the public taste is, therefore, improving.

And now our concerts in general, which seemed at one time to consult, rather than direct, the public taste, furnish us not only with every modern novelty, but frequently with the choicest specimens of ancient lore, known formerly to the musical antiquarian alone, or only heard by the subscribers to

* See page 125.

the concert of ancient music. The loss of
Salomon's concerts was amply supplied by the
by the establishment of the Philharmonic, directed (as all musical establishments ought to
be) by musicians alone. Here we have the
finest instrumental and vocal modern music.
Here the admirers of the German and Italian
schools meet, and learn to appreciate the opposite
merits of the beautiful and ornamental styles, with
a considerable, though inferior, portion of the
sublime; and how the ancient style would be
received, may be imagined from the extraordinary
applause excited by the occasional introduction
of a piece of this school on one or two occasions.

The Royal Academy of Music professes to
educate musicians on these principles. It employs masters in every style, Italian, German,
and English, for modern and ancient music;
and if this is kept up equally in all its departments, it cannot fail to diffuse a refined taste
throughout the world.

Another cause of the increase of taste is
the more general use, by our dilletante performers on the piano-forte, of music not ex-

pressly composed for that instrument, either
when read immediately from the score, or
from a correct adaptation. The productions
expressly intended for the piano-forte, or the
songs, with an accompaniment for that instrument alone, form but a very small part of
the ample abundance of what is admirable in
our art. A keyed instrument was originally
intended to be a guide to many parts, as
was the case with the organ. The peculiar
qualities of the harp, harpsichord, and piano-
forte, naturally suggested the invention and
cultivation of a style calculated to display their
tone and expression. Yet the great length of
time bestowed on the acquirement of execution
necessarily prevents the amateur from being
a good sight player, from studying score, and
becoming well acquainted with good music in
general; hence so many ladies, who, in their
earlier years, had acquired a brilliant finger,
and what is called a command of the instrument,
finding that they cannot continue music without
the assistance of a master, lay it wholly aside
in disgust. Their judgment and taste have never

been interested, they have never thoroughly understood or enjoyed the art. Let, however, the keyed instrument become a little domestic orchestra, and it will be constantly resorted to as reminding us of all that has delighted us in the church, oratorio, opera, and concert. And it is not only from the quantity and variety, but from the quality of the pieces, that the gratification will be enhanced ; for, as a general position, it may be asserted that the greatest masters have produced finer music for a full band than for any single instrument. Playing from score will, therefore, amply repay the time bestowed upon its acquirement. But it is not necessary that this difficulty should be surmounted by all who can play well ; for good adaptations of full vocal and instrumental music are, of late, greatly increased. Formerly adaptations were very ill executed ; skill and fidelity were required ; skill was often wanting, but fidelity, the more valuable of the two, was rarely met with. Adaptations were, indeed, seldom made by the authors themselves, but by a very inferior sort of musicians, who, instead of assuming the character of faithful translators, altered the original in every possible way, having perhaps what they deemed a sufficient reason for every alteration they made, though they ought not, if they could have avoided it, to have made one.

Another cause of the improvement of the public taste is the reprinting of what may be called classical music, undertaken, as it has been, in some instances, by the best musicians of the age.* The publication of sinfonias, quartetts, and operas in full score, is a proof of the existence of good taste on the Continent, as the importation, adaptation, and study of them will be of the improving taste of this nation.

One more cause only shall be mentioned, and that may appear to be a contradiction of a position just assumed, that piano-forte music is generally inferior to full music. But within a few years an improvement has gradually manifested itself in this department, the natural conse-

* Clementi's Practical Harmony; Bach's Fugues, by Wesley; Latrobe's Selection; the Fitzwilliam Collection; and Purcell's Sacred Music, by Novello, &c. &c.

quence of the increasing admiration of full music. In some few works intended as studies for this instrument\*, the exercises, instead of consisting, as formerly, wholly of passages of execution, and the ornamental fascinations of melody alone, to give rapidity to the finger, now prepare the eye, the hand, and the mind for score, directing them to harmony and science. I must not, however, be misunderstood, as if, after admitting that modern instrumental music is improved by the study of the peculiar characters of the several instruments, I made an exception to that of the pianoforte. Let, therefore, airs with variations, and fantasias, and whatever will contribute to the acquirement of execution and touch, be duly studied. The neatness of execution which they are meant to display, and the novelties and eccentricities with which they abound, will surprise and amuse us as long as they are new. But in reviewing and weighing their merits (of course I except those of the greatest composers), how

---

\* The Gradus ad Parnassum of Clementi; the Dulce et Utile of Cramer, and his Studios, &c. &c.

little is there for the mind to dwell on, how
little that will bear deliberate scrutiny, how
little that we should wish to hear repeated if
performed by a machine instead of a musician!
The piano-forte is now less frequently heard
with accompaniments than formerly. When
it is to be accompanied, perhaps the quality
of the instrument should be more studied
by the composer than when played by itself,
though Haydn, Mozart, and Beethoven did
not seem to think this a matter of importance, and often gave the same passage unaltered, alternately to each instrument. But
the piano-forte is now generally heard alone;
and the deficiency of its powers in sustaining
the sound, if not compared with other instruments, is less obvious, and is readily passed over.
Composers of solos for other instruments seem
anxious to combine every possible variety of
style and expression, while those who write for
the piano-forte seem afraid of exposing its defects, and accordingly display nothing but its
peculiarities. But if we consider this instrument as an amusement for home and solitude,

we cannot consent to give up the sublime and beautiful for the ornamental alone ; to neglect the higher and cultivate only the lower walks of the art. Played on the piano-forte, every species of music, both vocal and instrumental, ancient and modern, sacred and secular, may be more or less enjoyed. The imagination readily supplies the absent words of a finale or chorus previously heard at the opera or oratorio. The piano-forte seems to speak, and the qualities and tones of different instruments seem almost distinguishable.

The result, then, of these statements, is, that the public taste of this nation is in a gradual state of improvement; and, notwithstanding the decline of the art itself, which has been shown in a former part of this work, has attained a higher stage of advancement than it has known for half a century.

# INDEX

OF

# AUTHORS QUOTED.

---

# INDEX

## THE NAMES OF COMPOSERS.

---

# GENERAL INDEX.

# LIST OF PUBLICATIONS

BY

# DR. CROTCH,

*To be had at the Royal Harmonic Institution, Regent Street.*

---

|  | £ | s. | d. |
|---|---|---|---|
| MOTETT, " Methinks I hear," with new instrumental Accompaniments. | 0 | 4 | 0 |
| Overture and Finale, La Clemenza di Tito, Mozart, adapted as a Duet for the Piano-forte on a new plan | 0 | 3 | 6 |
| The same, arranged in the usual way | 0 | 4 | 0 |
| Sinfonia No. 2., as a Duet, composed by Dr. Crotch | 0 | 7 | 6 |
| ———— No. 7., Salomon's set, Haydn, as a Duet | 0 | 6 | 0 |
| ———— No. 8 | 0 | 6 | 0 |
| ———— No. 10 | 0 | 6 | 0 |
| Overture, Zauberflöte, Mozart; Duet | 0 | 3 | 6 |
| Sinfonia in C (Jupiter), Mozart; Duet | 0 | 8 | 0 |
| Nos. 1, 2, 3, 4, 5., constituting the First Act of Don Giovanni, Mozart, for the Piano-forte and Flute, each | 0 | 5 | 0 |
| Ditto, as a Duet, each | 0 | 6 | 0 |
| Preludes for the Piano-forte, and Instructions | 0 | 8 | 0 |
| Practical Thorough Bass | 0 | 12 | 0 |
| Fugue on a Subject of Three Notes | 0 | 1 | 0 |
| Divertimento for the Piano-forte, No. 1 | 0 | 2 | 6 |
| ————————————— No. 2 | 0 | 2 | 6 |
| ————————————— No. 3 | | | |

|                                                                                                      | £  | s. | d. |
|------------------------------------------------------------------------------------------------------|----|----|----|
| Anthem, Dr. Greene, " Sing unto the Lord," No. 1. (to be continued)                                   | 0  | 3  | 6  |
| Specimens of the various Kinds of Music performed in Dr. Crotch's Lectures, for the Pianoforte, 3 vols., each | 1  | 5  | 0  |
| Appendix to ditto, separate                                                                           | 0  | 4  | 0  |
| Palestine, a sacred Oratorio, the Words by the late Bishop Heber, the Voice Parts in Score, the Instrumental Parts adapted for the Pianoforte | 2  | 2  | 0  |
| The Overture, Choruses, &c. in Palestine, arranged by the Author as Duets for the Pianoforte          |    |    |    |
| Questions in Harmony, with their Answers, for the Examination of Young Pupils                         | 0  | 3  | 6  |
| Twelve Sinfonias, Haydn; Piano-forte, with Accompaniments for the Violin and Violoncello, each        | 0  | 5  | 0  |
| First Concerto, Corelli; Piano-forte                                                                  | 0  | 2  | 6  |
| " Cruda Sorte," Rossini, as a Duet                                                                    | 0  | 3  | 0  |
| Ditto,                single                                                                          | 0  | 2  | 0  |
| Finale to Der Freischutz, Weber                                                                       | 0  | 2  | 6  |
| Finale to the First Act of Il Matrimonio Segreto, Cimarosa, as a Duet                                 | 0  | 5  | 0  |
| Coro dello Sbarco, Il Crociato, Meyerbeer; Duet                                                       | 0  | 3  | 0  |
| Giovinetto Cavalier, from ditto; Duet                                                                 | 0  | 2  | 0  |
| Sinfonia Kozeluch in F; Piano-forte, with Accompaniments for the Violin and Violoncello               | 0  | 5  | 0  |
| Part of Sinfonia in A, Beethoven; Duet                                                                | 0  | 4  | 0  |
| Sinfonia Pastorale, Beethoven; Piano-forte, with Accompaniments for the Violin and Violoncello        | 0  | 10 | 6  |
| Three Duets, arranged from the Sonatas of Boccherini, as Duets, each                                  | 0  | 5  | 0  |
| Airs from Rousseau's Le Devin du Village; Duet                                                        | 0  | 4  | 0  |

| | | £ | s. | d. |
|---|---|---|---|---|
| Divertimento, Mozart, from a Quintett in D; Piano-forte | | 0 | 3 | 0 |
| " Cinto di nuovi allori," Rossini ; Duet | | 0 | 2 | 0 |

---

## OTHER PUBLICATIONS, BY THE SAME AUTHOR.

*To be had of Messrs. Lonsdale and Co., Chappell, the Author, &c. &c.*

| | | | |
|---|---|---|---|
| Three Sonatas | 0 | 7 | 6 |
| Ten Anthems, in Score | 0 | 10 | 6 |
| Ode to Fancy, in Score, an Exercise for his Doctor's Degree | 1 | 1 | 0 |
| Motett, 5 Voices, " Methinks I hear " | 0 | 2 | 6 |
| Glee, 4 Voices, " Go, tuneful Bird" | 0 | 1 | 0 |
| ——, 3 Voices, " To love thee, O my Emma"... | 0 | 1 | 0 |
| Ode, 5 Voices, " Mona on Snowdon calls " | 0 | 2 | 6 |
| Tallis's Latin Litany and old Psalm Tunes, in Score | 0 | 6 | 0 |
| No. 1. Original Airs for the Piano-forte, by John and William Crotch | 0 | 2 | 6 |
| 2. | 0 | 2 | 6 |
| 3. | 0 | 2 | 6 |
| No. 1. Organ Concerto | 0 | 5 | 0 |
| 2. Ditto | 0 | 6 | 0 |
| 3. Ditto | 0 | 7 | 6 |
| Organ Fugue, on a subject by Muffatt | 0 | 2 | 0 |
| Glee, 4 Voices, " Nymph, with thee" | 0 | 1 | 0 |
| Canzonet, " Clear shines the Sky " | 0 | 1 | 6 |
| Prelude and Air, with Variations ; Piano-forte | 0 | 1 | 6 |
| Glee, 4 Voices, " Yield thee to Pleasure" | 0 | 1 | 6 |
| Sonata, Piano-forte, in E♭ | 0 | 4 | 0 |
| Glee, 5 Voices, " Sweet Sylvan Scenes" | 0 | 1 | 6 |
| ——, 4 Voices, " Hail all the dear delights" | 0 | 2 | 0 |
| ——, 4 Voices, " Hail, Sympathy " | 0 | 3 | 0 |

|  | £ | s. | d. |
|---|---|---|---|
| Air, "Milton Oysters," with Variations; Piano-forte | 0 | 1 | 6 |
| Fantasia, Piano-forte | 0 | 2 | 0 |
| No. 1. Concerto, Mozart | 0 | 5 | 0 |
| 2. | 0 | 5 | 0 |
| 3. | 0 | 5 | 0 |
| Concerto, Dussek (Plough Boy) | | | |

The Overtures, Choruses, Marches, Sinfonias, &c. in Handel's Oratorios, Te Deums, Anthems, Operas, &c.

|  | £ | s. | d. |
|---|---|---|---|
| No. 1. Esther | 0 | 7 | 6 |
| 2. Deborah | 0 | 7 | 6 |
| 3. Athalia | 0 | 7 | 6 |
| 4. Acis and Galatea | 0 | 6 | 0 |
| 5. Alexander's Feast | 0 | 7 | 6 |
| 6. Dryden's Ode, "From Harmony" | 0 | 5 | 0 |
| 7. Israel in Egypt | 0 | 10 | 6 |
| 8. L'Allegro ed il Pensieroso | 0 | 5 | 0 |
| 9. Saul | 0 | 10 | 6 |
| 10. Messiah | 0 | 10 | 6 |
| 11. Samson | 0 | 7 | 6 |
| 12. Semele | 0 | 7 | 6 |
| 13. Belshazzar | 0 | 7 | 6 |
| 14. Susanna | 0 | 7 | 6 |
| 15. Six Oboe Concertos | 0 | 10 | 6 |
| 16. Hercules | 0 | 7 | 6 |
| 17. Occasional Oratorio | 0 | 6 | 0 |
| 18. The Choice of Hercules | 0 | 4 | 0 |
| 19. The 12 Grand Concertos, Book I. | 0 | 10 | 6 |
| 20. ———————————— II. | 0 | 10 | 6 |
| 21. Joseph | 0 | 7 | 6 |
| 22. Judas Macchabæus | 0 | 10 | 6 |
| 23. Joshua | 0 | 7 | 6 |
| 24. Alexander Balus | 0 | 6 | 0 |
| 25. The 4 Coronation Anthems | 0 | 7 | 6 |
| 26. Solomon | 0 | 10 | 6 |

To be continued.

|                                                                 | £ | s. | d. |
|-----------------------------------------------------------------|---|----|----|
| Quartett in C, Haydn; Piano-forte                               | 0 | 3  | 6  |
| ——— in E                                                        | 0 | 3  | 6  |
| Concerto in D, Geminiani; Piano-forte                           | 0 | 2  | 0  |
| Elements of Musical Composition and Thorough Bass               | 1 | 1  | 0  |
| Sinfonia, by Dr. C. in F, as a Duet, No. 1.                     | 0 | 8  | 0  |
| Romberg's Overture in D; Piano-forte                            | 0 | 2  | 6  |
| Thirty Rounds for the Piano-forte for learning to play from Score | 0 | 6  | 0  |
| Duet, The Hope of Israel, 2 Voices                              | 0 | 2  | 6  |
| Air, " Twilight," Miss Hamond, with Variations by Dr. C.        | 0 | 1  | 6  |
| " Una bella Serenata," and Finale, Così fan tutte, Mozart, as a Duet on a new plan | 0 | 3  | 0  |
| " Oh, quanto l'anima," Aria, by Meyer                           | 0 | 1  | 6  |
| " Ah, non Sai," Sarti                                           |   |    |    |
| " O Lord our Governor," Marcello                                | 0 | 2  | 0  |
| Anthem in Score, composed on the Death of the Duke of York      | 0 | 10 | 6  |

THE END.

LONDON:
Printed by A. & R. Spottiswoode,
New-Street-Square.

April **1842.**

# CATALOGUE OF NEW WORKS

PRINTED FOR

## LONGMAN, BROWN, & CO.

### London.

## № I.

COMPRISING

Wilson and Ogilvy, Printers,]      [57, Skinner Street, Snowhill.

# I. GEOGRAPHY, TOPOGRAPHY, VOYAGES AND TRAVELS, GUIDE BOOKS, &c.

## NOTES OF A TRAVELLER,
On the Social and Political State of France, Prussia, Switzerland, Italy, and other parts of Europe, during the present century. By SAMUEL LAING, Esq. 1 vol. 8vo. 16s. cloth lettered.

## JOURNAL OF A RESIDENCE IN NORWAY,
During the years 1834, 1835, and 1836; made with a view to inquire into the Rural and Political Economy of that Country, and the Condition of its Inhabitants. By SAMUEL LAING, Esq. 2d Edition, 1 vol. 8vo. 14s. cloth lettered.

## A TOUR IN SWEDEN,
In 1838; comprising observations on the Moral, Political, and Economical State of the Swedish Nation. By SAMUEL LAING, Esq. 1 vol. 8vo. 12s. cloth lettered.

## GREECE AS A KINGDOM:
A Statistical Description of that Country—its Laws, Commerce, Resources, Public Institutions, Army, Navy, &c.—from the arrival of King Otho, in 1833, down to the present time. From Official Documents and Authentic Sources. By FREDERICK STRONG, Esq. Consul at Athens for the Kingdoms of Bavaria and Hanover. 1 vol. 8vo 15s. cloth lettered.

## TRAVELS IN THE WEST:
Cuba, with Notices of Porto Rico and the Slave Trade. By D. TURNBULL, Esq. Member of the Royal Academy of History at Madrid, and of the Royal Patriotic and Economic Societies of Havana. 1 vol. 8vo. with Map, 15s. cloth lettered.

## MUSIC AND MANNERS IN FRANCE & NORTH GERMANY:
A series of Travelling Sketches of Art and Society. By H. F. CHORLEY, Esq. 3 vols. 31s. 6d.

## LOITERINGS OF TRAVEL:
A collection of Sketches of Manners, Incidents of Travel, Tales, and Poetry. By N. P. WILLIS, Esq. Author of "Pencillings by the Way," &c. 3 vols. post 8vo. £1. 11s. 6d. bds.

## THE MOUNTAINS AND LAKES OF SWITZERLAND:
With descriptive Sketches of other parts of the Continent. By Mrs. BRAY, Authoress of "Trials of the Heart," &c. &c. 3 vols. post 8vo. £1. 11s. 6d. bds.

## SIR EDW. SEAWARD'S NARRATIVE OF HIS SHIPWRECK,
and consequent Discovery of certain Islands in the Caribbean Sea: with a detail of many extraordinary and highly-interesting Events in his Life, from 1733 to 1749, as written in his own Diary. Edited by Miss JANE PORTER. 3d Edition, with a New Nautical and Geographical Introduction, containing Extracts from a Paper by Mr. C. F. Collett, of the Royal Navy, identifying the islands described by Sir Edward Seaward. 2 vols. post 8vo. 21s. cloth lettered.

## SKETCHES IN ERRIS AND TYRAWLY.
By the Rev. CÆSAR OTWAY. Post 8vo. with Map, and other Illustrations, 10s. 6d. cloth lett'd.

## A TOUR IN CONNAUGHT;
Comprising Sketches of Clonmacnoise, Joyce Country, and Achill. By the Rev. C. OTWAY. Fcp. 8vo. with Illustrations, 7s. 6d. cloth lettered.

## SKETCHES IN IRELAND,
Descriptive of interesting portions of the counties of Donegal, Cork, and Kerry. By the Rev. CÆSAR OTWAY. 2d Edition, corrected, 1 vol. fcp. 8vo. 6s. cloth lettered.

## A DICTIONARY, GEOGRAPHICAL, STATISTICAL, AND
HISTORICAL, of the various Countries, Places, and principal Natural Objects in the World. Illustrated with Maps. By J. R. M'CULLOCH, Esq. 2 vols. 8vo. £4. bound in cloth and lettered. Vol. 2 will be ready in the Spring. Parts 1 to 4 may be had, 5s. each: to be completed in Sixteen Parts.

## AN ENCYCLOPÆDIA OF GEOGRAPHY;
Comprising a complete History of the Earth; exhibiting its Relation to the Heavenly Bodies, its Physical Structure, the Natural History of each Country, and the Industry, Commerce, Political Institutions, and Civil and Social State of all Nations. By HUGH MURRAY, F.R.S.E. New edition, brought down to 1840, with 82 Maps, drawn by Sidney Hall, and upwards of 1000 other Engravings on Wood, from drawings by Swainson, T. Landseer, Sowerby, Strutt, &c., representing the most remarkable Objects of Nature and Art in every Region of the Globe. 1 very thick vol. 8vo. containing upwards of 1500 pages, £3. cloth lettered.

## THE HISTORY OF MARITIME AND INLAND DISCOVERY.
By W. D. COOLEY, Esq. 3 vols. fcp. 8vo. with Vignette Titles, 18s. cloth lettered.

## NARRATIVE OF A VOYAGE TO MADEIRA, TENERIFFE,
and along the Shores of the MEDITERRANEAN; including a Visit to Algiers, Egypt, Palestine, Tyre, Rhodes, Telmessus, Cyprus, and Greece, &c. &c. By W. R. WILDE, M.R.I.A. 2 vols. 8vo. with 30 Illustrations 28s. cloth.

**Geography, Topography, Voyages and Travels, Guide Books, &c.**

# A SYSTEM OF UNIVERSAL GEOGRAPHY,

Founded on the Works of MALTE-BRUN and BALBI, embracing an Historical Sketch of the Progress of Geographical Discovery, the Principles of Mathematical and Physical Geography, and a complete Description, from the most recent sources, of the Political and Social Condition of all the Countries in the World : with numerous Statistical Tables, and an Alphabetical Index of 12,000 Names. 1 thick vol. 8vo. closely and beautifully printed, 30s. strongly bound in cloth.

Although the names of Malte-Brun and Balbi have been annexed to the present work, in consequence of its forming a digest of all the very valuable information embraced by the respective "Systems" of these distinguished geographers, yet the variety and extent of original matter which has been introduced into its pages would fully justify its being entitled an entirely new work. The Political Geography, together with the Descriptive, Topographical, and Statistical departments, have been contributed by the Editors, Mr. Hugh Smith and Mr. James Lawrie ; in the departments of Mathematical and Physical Geography they have been assisted by J. P. Nichol, LL.D. F.R.S.E., Thos. Galloway, M.A. F.R.S., R. Hamilton, M.D. F.R.S.E., and J. H. Balfour, M.D. F.R.S.E.

# NEW GENERAL ATLAS OF FIFTY-THREE MAPS,

on Colombier Paper; with the Divisions and Boundaries carefully coloured. Constructed entirely from New Drawings, and engraved by SIDNEY HALL. New Edition, thoroughly revised and corrected to 1841 ; including all the Alterations rendered necessary by the recent Official Surveys, the New Roads on the Continent, and a careful Comparison with the authenticated Discoveries published in the latest Voyages and Travels. Folded in half, Nine Guineas, half-bound in russia ; full size of the Maps, Ten Pounds, half-bound in russia.

The following Maps have been re-engraved, from entirely new designs---Ireland, South Africa, Turkey in Asia ; the following have been materially improved---Switzerland, North Italy, South Italy, Egypt, Central Germany, Southern Germany, Greece, Austria, Spain and Portugal; a new Map of China, corrected from the recent government survey of the coast from Canton to Nankin (to which is appended, the Province of Canton, on an enlarged scale, in a separate compartment), has since been added.

# A SKETCH OF ANCIENT AND MODERN GEOGRAPHY.

By SAMUEL BUTLER, D.D. late Lord Bishop of Lichfield and Coventry; and formerly Head Master of Shrewsbury School. New Edition, revised by his SON, 8vo. 9s. bds.

The present edition has been carefully revised by the author's son, and such alterations introduced as continually-progressive discoveries and the latest information rendered necessary. Recent Travels have been constantly consulted where any doubt or difficulty seemed to require it; and some additional matter has been added, both in the ancient and modern part.

# ATLAS OF MODERN GEOGRAPHY.

By the late Dr. BUTLER. New Edition; consisting of Twenty-three coloured Maps, from a New Set of Plates. 8vo. with Index, 12s. half-bound.

# ATLAS OF ANCIENT GEOGRAPHY;

Consisting of Twenty-three coloured Maps. With Index. By the late Dr. BUTLER. New Edition. 8vo. 12s. half-bound.

\*\*\* The above two Atlases may be had, half-bound, in One Volume, in 4to. price 24s.

# BRITISH ATLAS OF FORTY-SEVEN MAPS,

CAREFULLY COLOURED; comprising separate Maps of every County in England, each Riding in Yorkshire, and North and South Wales; showing the Roads, Railways, Canals, Parks, Boundaries of Boroughs, Places of Election, Polling Places, &c. Compiled from the Maps of the Board of Ordnance and other Trigonometrical Surveys. By J. and C. WALKER. Imperial 4to. coloured, Three Guineas, half-bound ; large paper, Four Guineas, half-bound.

\*\*\* Each County may be had separately, in case, 2s. 6d.

# GUIDE TO ALL THE WATERING & SEA-BATHING PLACES

of Great Britain ; containing full and accurate Descriptions of each place, and of the Curiosities and striking Objects in the Environs ; and forming an agreeable and useful Companion during a residence at any of the places, or during a summer tour in quest of health or pleasure: with a Description of the Lakes, and a Tour through Wales. New Edition, including the SCOTCH WATERING PLACES, 1 thick vol. 18mo. illustrated by 94 Views and Maps, 15s. bound.

# THE ORIGINAL PICTURE OF LONDON :

With a Description of its Environs. Re-edited, and mostly re-written, by J. BRITTON, F.S.A. &c. 28th Edition, with upwards of 100 Views of Public Buildings, Plan of the Streets, and Two Maps, 18mo. 9s. neatly bound; with the Maps only, 6s. bound.

# NICHOLSON'S CAMBRIAN TRAVELLER'S GUIDE

In every direction ; containing Remarks made during many Excursions in the Principality of Wales. 3d Edition, revised and corrected by his Son, the Rev. E. NICHOLSON, Incumbent of Minsterley, Salop, 1 thick vol. 8vo. 20s. cloth lettered.

# THE WYE AND ITS ASSOCIATIONS :

A Narrative of a Pedestrian Ramble. By LEITCH RITCHIE, Esq. Author of "Wanderings by the Loire," "Wanderings by the Seine," &c. &c. 1 vol. crown 8vo. with 12 highly-finished Engravings, after Sketches by T. Creswick, 12s. cloth lettered.

# ITALY AND ITS COMFORTS :

A Manual for Tourists. By M. VALERY, Author of "Travels in Corsica, Elba, Sardinia," &c. 1 vol. 12mo. with an Index Map, 7s. 6d. cloth.

## II. HISTORY AND BIOGRAPHY.

### THE HISTORY OF ENGLAND,

From the Earliest Period to the Death of Elizabeth. By SHARON TURNER, Esq. F.A.S. R.A.S.L. 12 vols. 8vo. £8. 3s. cloth lettered.

*The above may also be had in the following separate portions :—*

THE HISTORY of the ANGLO-SAXONS; comprising the History of England from the Earliest Period to the Norman Conquest. 5th Edition, 3 vols. 8vo. £2. 5s. bds.

THE HISTORY of ENGLAND during the MIDDLE AGES; comprising the Reigns from William the Conqueror to the Accession of Henry VIII,, and also the History of the Literature, Religion, Poetry, and Progress of the Reformation and of the Language during that period. 3d Edition, 5 vols. 8vo. £3, bds.

THE HISTORY of the REIGN of HENRY VIII.; comprising the Political History of the commencement of the English Reformation: being the First Part of the Modern History of England. 3d Edition, 2 vols. 8vo. 26s. bds.

THE HISTORY of the REIGNS of EDWARD VI., MARY, and ELIZABETH; being the Second Part of the Modern History of England. 2d Edition, 2 vols. 8vo. 32s. bds.

### BLAIR'S CHRONOLOGICAL AND HISTORICAL TABLES,

From the Creation to our time. New Edition, greatly improved, with Additions and Corrections from the most authentic Writers, printed in a more convenient form, in 1 vol. royal 8vo. —*In the spring.*

### THE GENERAL HISTORY OF THE WORLD,

From the earliest times until the year 1831. By CHARLES VON ROTTECK, LL.D. Professor in the University of Freiburg, Aulic Counsellor, Member of the Chamber of Deputies of the Grand Duchy of Baden, &c. Translated from the German, and continued to 1840. 4 vols. 8vo. £2, cloth lettered.

CONTENTS.

Introduction.—Of History in general.

First Book.—Ancient World: History from the Origin of Mankind, or from the Commencement of Historical Knowledge to the Migration of Nations—from A.M. 1 (or 3983 B.C.) to A.D. 400.

Second Book.—Middle Ages: History from the Great Migration of Nations until the Discovery of both Indies and the Reformation—from A.D. 400 to 1500.

Third Book.—Modern History, First Part: History from the Discovery of America until the French Revolution—from A.D. 1492 to 1789.

Fourth Book.—Modern History, Second Part: From the Commencement of the French Revolution to the Present Time—1789 to 1840.

Appendix, containing a general View of the principal Events from the Foundation of the Holy Alliance till the last French Revolution (1830).

\*\*\* Each Volume contains a Table of Synchronal Events.

### LIFE OF FREDERICK THE SECOND, KING OF PRUSSIA.

By LORD DOVER. 2d Edition, 2 vols. 8vo. with Portrait, 28s. bds.

### ECCLESIASTICAL CHRONOLOGY;

Or, Annals of the Christian Church, from its Foundation to the present Time. Containing a View of General Church History, and the Course of Secular Events; the Limits of the Church and its Relations to the State; Controversies; Sects and Parties; Rites, Institutions, and Discipline ; Ecclesiastical Writers. The whole arranged according to the order of Dates, and divided into Seven Periods. To which are added, Lists of Councils and Popes, Patriarchs, and Archbishops of Canterbury. By the Rev. J. E. RIDDLE, M.A., Author of "The Complete Latin Dictionary." 1 vol. 8vo. 15s. cloth lettered.

### A HISTORY OF THE LIFE OF EDWARD THE BLACK

PRINCE, and of Various Events connected therewith, which occurred during the Reign of Edward III. King of England. By G. P. R. JAMES, Esq. 2d Edition, 2 vols. fcp. 8vo. with Map, 15s. cloth lettered.

### THE HISTORY OF CHARLEMAGNE;

With a Sketch of the State and History of France from the Fall of the Roman Empire to the Rise of the Carlovingian Dynasty. By G. P. R. JAMES, Esq. 1 vol. 8vo. with Portraits, &c. 16s. boards.

## History and Biography.

### THE HISTORY OF RUSSIA,
From the Earliest Period to the Treaty of Tilsit.  By ROBERT BELL, Esq.  3 vols. fcp. 8vo.
with Vignette Titles, 18s. cloth lettered.

### THE HISTORY OF SPAIN AND PORTUGAL.
By Dr. DUNHAM.  5 vols. fcp. 8vo. with Vignette Titles, £1. 10s. cloth lettered.

### THE HISTORY OF EUROPE DURING THE MIDDLE AGES.
By Dr. DUNHAM.  4 vols. fcp. 8vo. with Vignette Titles, £1. 4s. cloth lettered.

### THE HISTORY OF THE ITALIAN REPUBLICS;
Or, of the Origin, Progress, and Fall of Freedom in Italy, from A.D. 476 to 1805.  By J. C. L.
de SISMONDI.  2 vols. fcp. 8vo. with Vignette Titles, 12s. cloth lettered.

### THE HISTORY OF THE FALL OF THE ROMAN EMPIRE;
Comprising a View of the Invasion and Settlement of the Barbarians.  by J.C L. de SISMONDI.
2 vols. fcp. 8vo. with Vignette Titles, 12s. cloth lettered.

### THE HISTORY OF ROME.
2 vols. fcp. 8vo. 12s. cloth lettered.

### THE HISTORY OF GREECE.
By the Right Rev. the LORD BISHOP of ST. DAVID'S.  Vols. 1 to 7, fcp. 8vo. with Vignette
Titles, £2. 2s. cloth lettered.

### A TREATISE ON THE ARTS, MANNERS, MANUFACTURES,
and INSTITUTIONS of the GREEKS and ROMANS.  By the Rev. T. D. FOSBROKE, &c. &c.
2 vols. fcp. 8vo. with Vignette Titles, 12s. cloth lettered.

### THE HISTORY OF THE CHRISTIAN CHURCH,
From its Foundation to A.D. 1492.  By the Rev. H. STEBBING, M.A. &c.  2 vols. fcp. 8vo.
with Vignette Titles, 12s. cloth lettered.

### THE HISTORY OF THE REFORMATION.
By the Rev. H. STEBBING.  2 vols. fcp. 8vo. with Vignette Titles, 12s. cloth lettered.

### THE HISTORY OF MARITIME AND INLAND DISCOVERY.
By W. D. COOLEY, Esq.  3 vols. fcp. 8vo. with Vignette Titles, 18s. cloth lettered.

### THE CHRONOLOGY OF HISTORY.
Containing Tables, Calculations, and Statements indispensable for ascertaining the Dates of
Historical Events, and of Public and Private Documents, from the Earliest Period to the
Present Time.  By Sir HARRIS NICOLAS, K.C. M.G.  Second edition, corrected throughout.
1 vol. fcp. 8vo. with Vignette Title, 6s. cloth lettered.

### THE STATESMEN OF THE COMMONWEALTH OF ENGLAND.
With an Introductory Treatise on the Popular Progress in English History.  By JOHN
FORSTER, Esq.  5 vols. fcp. 8vo. with Original Portraits of Pym, Eliot, Hampden, Cromwell,
and an Historical Scene after a Picture by Cattermole, £1. 10s. cloth lettered.

The Introductory Treatise, intended as an Introduction to the Study of the Great Civil War in
the Seventeenth Century, may be had separately, price 2s. 6d.

The above 5 vols. form Mr. Forster's portion of the Lives of Eminent British Statesmen, by Sir
James Mackintosh, the Right Hon. T. P. Courtenay, and John Forster, Esq.  7 vols. fcp. 8vo.
with Vignette Titles, £2. 2s. cloth lettered.

### LIVES OF THE MOST EMINENT ENGLISH POETS.
By ROBERT BELL, Esq.  2 vols. fcp. 8vo. with Vignette Titles, 12s. cloth lettered.

### THE HISTORY OF DENMARK, SWEDEN, AND NORWAY.
By Dr. DUNHAM.  3 vols. fcp. 8vo. with Vignette Titles, 18s. cloth lettered.

### THE HISTORY OF POLAND.
By Dr. DUNHAM.  1 vol. fcp. 8vo. with Vignette Title, 6s. cloth lettered.

### THE LIVES OF THE EARLY WRITERS OF GREAT BRITAIN.
By Dr. DUNHAM, R. BELL, Esq. &c. &c.  1 vol. fcp. 8vo. with Vignette Title, 6s. cloth
lettered.

### LIVES OF EMINENT BRITISH LAWYERS.
By HENRY ROSCOE, Esq.  1 vol. fcp. 8vo. with Vignette Title, 6s. cloth lettered.

## History and Biography.

### OUTLINES OF HISTORY,

From the Earliest Period. By THOMAS KEIGHTLEY, Esq. New Edition, corrected and considerably improved, fcp. 8vo. 6s. cloth lettered; or 6s. 6d. bound and lettered.

### THE HISTORY OF ENGLAND.

By THOMAS KEIGHTLEY, Esq. In 2 vols. 12mo. in cloth, 14s.; or bound, 15s.
For the convenience of Schools, the volumes will always be sold separately.

### AN ELEMENTARY HISTORY OF ENGLAND.

By THOMAS KEIGHTLEY, Esq., Author of "A History of England," "Greece," "Rome," "Outlines of History," &c. &c. 12mo. bound and lettered, 5s.

This book has been compiled in consequence of numerous complaints of the ordinary School Histories, addressed to the author by several persons of both sexes engaged in the task of education. They state, that the abridgments are, almost without exception, so dry and uninteresting, as to be utterly distasteful to children; that they contain matter far beyond their comprehension, and are in some cases too long to be used with advantage. In the present Elementary History it is the object of the author to avoid all these faults. The work is brought within the most moderate compass, and nothing is introduced into it that is not likely to prove both intelligible and interesting to children under the age of ten or eleven years, for whose use it is designed.

### THE HISTORY OF GREECE.

By THOMAS KEIGHTLEY, Esq. Third edition, 12mo. 6s. 6d. cloth, or 7s. bound.

ELEMENTARY HISTORY of GREECE, 18mo. 3s. 6d. bound.

### THE HISTORY OF ROME

To the end of the Republic. By THOMAS KEIGHTLEY, Esq. Third edition, 12mo. 6s. 6d. or 7s. bound.

ELEMENTARY HISTORY of ROME, 18mo. 3s. 6d. bound.

### THE HISTORY OF THE ROMAN EMPIRE,

From the Accession of Augustus to the end of the Empire in the West. By T. KEIGHTLEY, Esq. 12mo. 6s. 6d. cloth, or 7s. bound.

QUESTIONS on the HISTORIES of ENGLAND (2 Parts), ROME, and GREECE, 1s. each.

### THE BIOGRAPHICAL TREASURY:

A new and complete Dictionary of Universal Biography. Consisting of the Lives of above 12,000 eminent Persons from the Earliest Periods of History to the year 1841. By SAMUEL MAUNDER. New Edition, with Supplement. Fcp. 8vo. 8s. 6d. cloth lettered; or 10s. 6d. bound in roan with gilt edges.

### THE TREASURY OF HISTORY AND GEOGRAPHY;

Comprising a general introductory Outline of Universal History, ancient and modern, and a complete series of separate Histories of every Nation that exists or has existed in the World; in which is developed their Rise, Progress, and Present Condition; the Moral and Social Character of their respective Inhabitants, their Religion, Manners, and Customs; together with the Geographical Position and Commercial Advantages of each Country, their Natural Productions, and General Statistics. By SAMUEL MAUNDER. 1 vol. Fcp. 8vo.— (*In the press.*)

### THE HISTORY OF ENGLAND.

By Sir JAMES MACKINTOSH; W. WALLACE, Esq.; and ROBERT BELL, ESQ. 10 vols. fcp. 8vo. with Vignette Titles, £3. cloth lettered.

### THE HISTORY OF SCOTLAND.

By Sir WALTER SCOTT, Bart. New edition. 2 vols. fcp. 8vo. with Vignette Titles, 12s. cloth lettered.

### THE HISTORY OF IRELAND.

By THOMAS MOORE, Esq. Vols. 1 to 3, with Vignette Titles, 18s.

### THE HISTORY OF THE UNITED STATES OF AMERICA,

From the Discovery of America to the Election of General Jackson to the Presidency. By the Rev. H. FERGUS. 2 vols. fcp. 8vo. with Vignette Titles, 12s. cloth lettered.

### THE HISTORY OF FRANCE,

From the Earliest Period to the Abdication of Napoleon. By E. E. CROWE, Esq. 3 vols. fcp. 8vo. with Vignette Titles, 18s. cloth lettered.

### THE HISTORY OF THE NETHERLANDS,

From the Invasion by the Romans to the Belgian Revolution in 1830. By T. C. GRATTAN, Esq. 1 vol. fcp. 8vo. with Vignette Title, 6s. cloth lettered.

### THE HISTORY OF SWITZERLAND.

1 vol. fcp. 8vo. with Vignette Title, 6s. cloth lettered.

## History and Biography.

# HISTORICAL RECORDS OF THE BRITISH ARMY:

Comprising the History of every Regiment in Her Majesty's Service. By RICHARD CANNON, Esq., Adjutant-General's Office, Horse Guards.

The following are already published:

1. The LIFE GUARDS—Containing an account of the Formation of the Corps in the year 1660, and of its subsequent Services to 1836. Illustrated with Plates. 2d Edition, 8vo. 12s. boards.

2. The ROYAL REGIMENT OF HORSE GUARDS, or OXFORD BLUES—Its Services, and the transactions in which it has been engaged from its establishment in 1661, to the present time. By EDMUND PACKE, late Captain, Royal Horse Guards. With Plates, and Portrait of Aubrey de Vere, 20th Earl of Oxford, 1st Colonel of the Regiment. 8vo. 10s. cloth lettered.

3. The FIRST, or KING'S REGIMENT OF DRAGOON GUARDS—Containing an account of the Formation of the Regiment in 1685, and of its subsequent Services to 1835. Illustrated with Plates. 8vo. 8s. cloth lettered.

4. The SECOND, or QUEEN'S REGIMENT OF DRAGOON GUARDS (Queen's Bays)—Containing an account of the Formation of the Regiment in 1685, and of its subsequent Services to 1837. Illustrated with Plates. 8vo. 8s. cloth lettered.

5. The THIRD, or PRINCE OF WALES' REGIMENT OF DRAGOON GUARDS—Containing an account of the Formation of the Regiment in 1685, and of its subsequent Services to 1838. Illustrated with Plates. 8vo. 8s. in boards.

6. The FOURTH, or ROYAL IRISH REGIMENT OF DRAGOON GUARDS—Containing an account of the Formation of the Regiment in 1685, and of its subsequent Services to 1838. Illustrated with Plates. 8vo. 8s. cloth lettered.

7. The FIFTH, or PRINCESS CHARLOTTE OF WALES' REGIMENT OF DRAGOON GUARDS—Containing an account of the Formation of the Regiment in 1685, with its subsequent Services to 1838. Illustrated with Plates. 8vo. 8s. cloth lettered.

8. The SIXTH DRAGOON GUARDS. 8vo. 8s. cloth lettered.

9. The SEVENTH, or PRINCESS ROYAL'S REGIMENT OF DRAGOON GUARDS—Containing an account of the Formation of the Regiment in 1688, and of its subsequent Services to 1839. Illustrated with Plates. 8vo. 8s. cloth lettered.

10. The FIRST, or ROYAL REGIMENT OF DRAGOONS—Containing an account of its Formation in the Reign of King Charles the Second, and of its subsequent Services to 1839. Illustrated with Plates. 8vo. 8s. cloth lettered.

11. The ROYAL REGIMENT OF SCOTS DRAGOONS; now, The Second, or Royal North British Dragoons, commonly called The Scots Greys—Containing an account of the Formation of the Regiment in the Reign of King Charles the Second, and of its subsequent Services to 1839. Illustrated with Plates. 8vo. 8s. cloth lettered.

12. The FIRST, or ROYAL REGIMENT OF FOOT—Containing an account of the Origin of the Regiment in the Reign of King James the Sixth of Scotland, and of its subsequent Services to 1838. Illustrated with Plates. 8vo. 12s. cloth lettered.

13. The SECOND, or QUEEN'S ROYAL REGIMENT OF FOOT—Containing an account of the Formation of the Regiment in 1661, and of its subsequent Services to 1837. 8vo. 8s. bds.

14. The THIRD REGIMENT OF FOOT, or THE BUFFS; formerly designated the Holland Regiment—Containing an account of its Origin in the Reign of Queen Elizabeth, and of its subsequent Services to 1838. Illustrated with Plates. 8vo. 12s. boards.

15. The FOURTH, or KING'S OWN REGIMENT OF FOOT—Containing an account of the Formation of the Regiment in 1680, and its subsequent Service to 1839. Illustrated with Plates. 8vo. 8s. cloth lettered.

16. The FIFTH REGIMENT OF FOOT, or NORTHUMBERLAND FUSILEERS—Containing an account of the Formation of the Regiment in 1674, and of its subsequent Services to 1837. Illustrated with Plates. 8vo. 8s. cloth lettered.

17. The SIXTH, or ROYAL FIRST WARWICKSHIRE REGIMENT OF FOOT—Containing an account of the Formation of the Regiment in the year 1674, and of its subsequent Services to 1838. Illustrated with Plates. 8vo. 8s. cloth lettered.

18. The EIGHTY-EIGHTH REGIMENT OF FOOT, or CONNAUGHT RANGERS—Containing an account of the Formation of the Regiment in 1793, and of its subsequent Services to 1837. With Plate. 8vo. 6s. cloth lettered.

# LIVES OF THE MOST EMINENT BRITISH MILITARY

COMMANDERS. By the Rev. G. R. GLEIG. 3 vols. fcp. 8vo. with Vignette Titles, 18s. cloth lettered.

# LIVES OF THE BRITISH ADMIRALS;

with an Introductory View of the Naval History of England. By R. SOUTHEY, Esq. and R. BELL, Esq. 5 vols. fcp. 8vo. with Vignette Titles, £1. 10s. cloth lettered.

# THE HISTORY OF THE GERMANIC EMPIRE.

By Dr. DUNHAM. 3 vols. fcp. 8vo. with Vignette Titles, 18s. cloth lettered.

## History and Biography.

# LIVES OF THE MOST EMINENT FOREIGN STATESMEN.

By G. P. R. JAMES, Esq., and E. E. CROWE, Esq.   5 vols. fcp. 8vo. with Vignette Titles, 30s. cloth lettered.

# THE HISTORY OF THE KNIGHTS TEMPLARS,

The Temple Church, and the Temple. By C. G. ADDISON, of the Inner Temple. 2d Edition, enlarged, 1 vol. square crown 8vo. with Illustrations, 18s. cloth lettered.—(Just ready.)

This work forms a complete history of the Order of the Temple, from the time of its foundation in Palestine, to the period of its abolition by the Pope and the Council of Trent. A full and interesting account is given of the establishment of the Knights Templars in Great Britain, of the foundation of the Temple in London, and of the erection of the Temple Church.

# SIR HENRY CAVENDISH'S DEBATES OF THE HOUSE OF

COMMONS, during the Thirteenth Parliament of Great Britain, commonly called the Unreported Parliament. To which are appended, Illustrations of the Parliamentary History of the Reign of George III., consisting of Unpublished Letters, Private Journals, Memoirs, &c. Drawn up from the Original MSS., by J. WRIGHT, Esq., Editor of the Parliamentary History of England. In 4 vols. royal 8vo. Vol. 1 is now ready, 25s. in cloth lettered. This work is also published in Parts, 6s. each, of which four are now published.

It has often been regretted that the proceedings of the House of Commons, during the thirteenth Parliament of Great Britain, which met in May, 1768, and was dissolved in June, 1771, should, in consequence of the strict enforcement of the standing order for the exclusion of strangers from the gallery of the house, have remained nearly a blank in the history of the country. The debates of this period, were, however, fortunately taken down by a member of the house, Mr. Henry Cavendish, and the editor having discovered his MSS., and obtained permission to print them, they are now given to the world. The collection contains upwards of two hundred speeches by Burke, which have never seen the light; together with a number of the most valuable speeches of Mr. George Grenville, Lord North, Mr. Dunning, Mr. Thurlow, Mr. Wedderburn, Mr. Fox, Colonel Barré, Mr., afterwards Chief Justice, Blackstone, &c. &c. It embraces the whole of the stirring period of the publication of the Letters of Junius, and exhibits the feeling which prevailed in the House and in the country, previous to the unhappy contest which took place between Great Britain and her American Colonies.

# THE MILITARY LIFE OF FIELD-MARSHAL THE DUKE OF

WELLINGTON, K.G., &c. &c. By Major BASIL JACKSON, and Captain C. ROCHFORT SCOTT, late of the Royal Staff Corps. 2 vols. 8vo. with Portraits and numerous Plans of Battles, 30s. cloth lettered.

# THE LIFE OF THOMAS BURGESS, D.D. F.R.S. &c.

Late Lord Bishop of Salisbury. By JOHN S. HARFORD, Esq. D.C.L. F.L.S. 2d Edition, with additions, fcp. 8vo. with Portrait, 8s. 6d. cloth lettered.

# THE HISTORY OF THE PELOPONNESIAN WAR.

By THUCYDIDES. Newly Translated into English, and accompanied with very copious notes, Philological and Explanatory, Historical and Geographical. By the Rev. S. T. BLOOMFIELD, D.D. F.S.A. 3 vols. 8vo. with Maps and Plates, £2. 5s. boards.

# HISTORICAL AND MISCELLANEOUS QUESTIONS,

For the Use of Young People; with a Selection of British and General Biography. By R. MANGNALL. New Edition, with the Author's last Corrections and Additions, and other very considerable recent Improvements, 12mo. bound, 4s. 6d.

\*\*\* The only edition, with the Author's latest Additions and Improvements, bears the imprint of Messrs LONGMAN and Co.

# QUESTIONS ON THE HISTORY OF EUROPE;

A Sequel to Mangnall's Historical Questions: comprising Questions on the History of the Nations of Continental Europe not comprehended in that work. By JULIA CORNER. New Edition, 12mo. 5s. bound and lettered.

# THE NEW PANTHEON;

Or, an Introduction to the Mythology of the Ancients, in Question and Answer; compiled for the Use of Young Persons. To which are added, an Accentuated Index, Questions for Exercise, and Poetical Illustrations of Grecian Mythology, from Homer and Virgil. By W. J. HORT. New Edition, considerably enlarged by the addition of the Oriental and Northern Mythology, 18mo. 17 Plates, 5s. 6d. bound.

# AN INTRODUCTION TO THE STUDY OF CHRONOLOGY

And ANCIENT HISTORY. By W. J. HORT. New Edition, 18mo. 4s. bound.

# AN ABRIDGMENT OF UNIVERSAL HISTORY,

Adapted to the Use of Families and Schools; with appropriate Questions at the end of each Section. By the Rev. H. J. KNAPP, M.A. New Edition, with considerable additions, 12mo. 5s. bound.

# ON THE STUDY AND USE OF ANCIENT AND MODERN

HISTORY; containing Observations and Reflections on the Causes and Consequences of those Events which have produced conspicuous changes in the aspect of the World, and the general state of Human Affairs. In a Series of Letters. By JOHN BIGLAND, Author of "Letters on the Political State of Europe." 7th Edition, 1 vol. 12mo. 6s. boards.

## History and Biography.

### LIVES OF THE MOST EMINENT LITERARY MEN OF ITALY, SPAIN, and PORTUGAL.
By Mrs. SHELLEY, Sir D. BREWSTER, J. MONTGOMERY, &c. 3 vols. fcp. 8vo. with Vignette Titles, 18s. cloth lettered.

### THE LIVES OF BRITISH DRAMATISTS.
By Dr. DUNHAM, R. BELL, Esq. &c. 2 vols. fcp. 8vo. with Vignette Titles, 12s. cloth lettered.

### LIVES OF THE MOST EMINENT FRENCH WRITERS.
By Mrs. SHELLEY, and others. 2 vols. fcp. 8vo. with Vignette Titles, 12s. cloth lettered.

## III. NOVELS, TALES, &c.

### THE JACQUERIE;
Or, the Lady and the Page. By G. P. R. JAMES, Esq. 3 vols. post 8vo. £1. 11s. 6d.

### THE ANCIENT REGIME:
A Tale. By G. P. R. JAMES, Esq. 3 vols. post 8vo. £1. 11s. 6d.

### CORSE DE LEON;
Or the Brigand. By G. P. R. JAMES. Esq. 3 vols. post 8vo. £1. 11s. 6d.

### THE KING'S HIGHWAY:
A Novel. By G. P. R. JAMES, Esq. 3 vols. post 8vo. £1. 11s. 6d.

### HENRY OF GUISE;
Or, the States of Blois. By G. P. R. JAMES, Esq. 3 vols. post 8vo. £1. 11s. 6d.

### THE HUGUENOT:
A Tale of the French Protestants. By G. P. R. JAMES, Esq. 3 vols. post 8vo. 31s. 6d.

### THE GENTLEMAN OF THE OLD SCHOOL.
By G. P. R. JAMES, Esq. 3 vols. post 8vo. £1. 11s. 6d.

### THE ROBBER.
By G. P. R. JAMES, Esq. 2d Edition, 3 vols. post 8vo. £1. 11s. 6d.

### LIFE AND ADVENTURES OF JOHN MARSTON HALL.
By G. P. R. JAMES, Esq. 3 vols. post 8vo. £1. 11s. 6d.

### MARY OF BURGUNDY;
Or, the Revolt of Ghent. By G. P. R. JAMES, Esq. 3 vols. post 8vo. £1. 11s. 6d.

### ONE IN A THOUSAND;
Or, the Days of Henri-Quatre. By G. P. R. JAMES, Esq. 3 vols. post 8vo. £1. 11s. 6d.

### ATTILA:
A Romance. By G. P. R. JAMES, Esq. 3 vols. post 8vo. £1. 11s. 6d.

### THE DOCTOR, &c.
5 vols. post 8vo. £2. 12s. 6d. cloth.

### POOR JACK.
By Captain MARRYAT. 1 vol. medium 8vo. with above 40 Illustrations by Clarkson Stanfield, price 14s. cloth lettered.

### JOSEPH RUSHBROOK, THE POACHER.
By Captain MARRYAT. 3 vols. post 8vo. £1. 11s. 6d.

### JANE SINCLAIR;
Or, the Fawn of Spring Vale: Lha Dhu, or the Dark Day; the Clarionet; the Dead Boxer; the Misfortunes of Barney Branagan; the Resurrections of Barney Bradley. By WILLIAM CARLETON. 3 vols. post 8vo. £1. 11s. 6d. boards.

### FARDOROUGHA THE MISER;
Or, the Convicts of Lisnamona. By WILLIAM CARLETON. 2d Edition, fcp. 8vo. 6s. cloth.

### FATHER BUTLER AND THE LOUGH DERG PILGRIM.
By WILLIAM CARLETON. 2d Edition, fcp. 8vo. 3s. 6d. cloth.

## IV. ENCYCLOPÆDIAS AND DICTIONARIES.

### A DICTIONARY OF SCIENCE, LITERATURE, AND ART;

Comprising the History, Description, and Scientific Principles of every Branch of Human Knowledge; with the Derivation and Definition of all the Terms in General Use. Edited by W. T. Brande, F.R.S. L. and E.; assisted by Joseph Cauvin, Esq. The various departments are by Gentlemen of eminence in each. 1 very thick vol. 8vo. containing above 1400 closely printed pages, illustrated by Wood Engravings, £3. handsomely bound in cloth, and lettered. This work is also published in 12 parts, 5s. each, of which 11 have appeared.

### A DICTIONARY, GEOGRAPHICAL, STATISTICAL, AND

HISTORICAL, of the various Countries, Places, and Principal Natural Objects in the WORLD. Illustrated with Maps. By J. R. M'Culloch, Esq. 2 very thick vols. 8vo. £4. bound in cloth, and lettered. This work is also published in parts, 5s. each, of which 14 have appeared; to be completed in 2 more parts.

### A DICTIONARY OF COMMERCE AND COMMERCIAL NAVI-

GATION (Practical, Theoretical, and Historical.) With Maps and Plans. By J. R. M'Culloch, Esq. New Edition, with Supplement, £2. 10s. cloth lettered.

### ENCYCLOPÆDIA OF GEOGRAPHY;

Comprising a complete Description of the Earth: exhibiting its Relation to the Heavenly Bodies, its Physical Structure, the Natural History of each Country, and the Industry, Commerce, Political Institutions, and Civil and Social State of all Nations. By Hugh Murray, F.R.S.E.: assisted in Astronomy, &c. by Professor Wallace; Geology, &c. by Professor Jameson; Botany, &c. by Sir W. J. Hooker; Zoology, &c. by W. Swainson, Esq. New Edition, brought down to 1840: with 82 Maps, drawn by Sidney Hall, and upwards of 1000 other Engravings on Wood, from Drawings by Swainson, T. Landseer, Sowerby, Strutt, &c. representing the most remarkable Objects of Nature and Art in every Region of the Globe. 1 vol. 8vo. containing upwards of 1500 pages, £3, cloth.

### AN ENCYCLOPÆDIA OF RURAL SPORTS;

Or, a complete Account, Historical, Practical, and Descriptive, of Hunting, Shooting, Fishing, Racing, and other Field Sports and Athletic Amusements of the present day. By Delabere P. Blaine, Esq., Author of "Outlines of the Veterinary Art," "Canine Pathology," &c. &c. Illustrated by nearly 600 Engravings on Wood, by R. Branston, from Drawings by Alken, T. Landseer, Dickes, &c. 1 very thick vol. 8vo. £2. 10s. handsomely bound in fancy cloth, lettered.

### AN ENCYCLOPÆDIA OF GARDENING;

Comprising the Theory and Practice of Horticulture, Floriculture, Arboriculture, and Landscape Gardening, including all the latest improvements, a General History of Gardening in all Countries, and a Statistical View of its Present State, with Suggestions for its Future Progress in the British Isles. By J. C. Loudon, F.L.S. H.S. &c. New Edition, greatly enlarged and improved, in 1 very thick vol. 8vo. with nearly 1000 engravings on Wood, £2. 10s. cloth lettered.

### AN ENCYCLOPÆDIA OF PLANTS;

Comprising the Description, Specific Character, Culture, History, Application in the Arts, and every other desirable particular, respecting all the Plants Indigenous to, Cultivated in, or Introduced into Britain; combining all the advantages of a Linnæan and Jussieuan Species Plantarum, an Historia Plantarum, a Grammar of Botany, and a Dictionary of Botany and Vegetable Culture. The whole in English, with the Synonymes of the commoner Plants in the different European and other languages; the scientific names accentuated, their etymology explained; the Classes, Orders, and Botanic Terms illustrated by engravings; and with Figures of nearly 10,000 species, exemplifying several Individuals belonging to every genus included in the work. Edited by J. C. Loudon, F.L.S. H.S. &c.: the Specific Characters by Professor Lindley; the Drawings by J. D. C. Sowerby, F.L.S.; and the Engravings by R. Branston. 2d Edition, corrected, with Supplement, in 1 very thick vol. 8vo. £3. 13s. 6d. cloth lettered.

### AN ENCYCLOPÆDIA OF AGRICULTURE.

By J. C. Loudon, F.L.S. H.S. &c. Comprising the Theory and Practice of the Valuation, Transfer, Laying out, Improvement, and Management of Landed Property, and the Cultivation and Economy of the Animal and Vegetable Productions of Agriculture, including the latest Improvements, a General History of Agriculture in all Countries, and a Statistical View of its Present State, with Suggestions for its Future Progress. With nearly 1,300 Engravings on Wood. 3d Edition, with a Supplement, containing all the recent Improvements, in 1 very thick vol. 8vo. £2. 10s. cloth lettered.

### A DICTIONARY OF PRINTING.

By William Savage, Author of "Practical Hints on Decorative Printing," and a Treatise "On the Preparation of Printing Ink, both Black and Coloured." In 1 vol. 8vo. with numerous Diagrams, £1. 6s. cloth lettered.

## Encyclopædias and Dictionaries.

### A DICTIONARY OF ARTS, MANUFACTURES, AND MINES;
Containing a clear Exposition of their Principles and Practice. By ANDREW URE, M.D.
F.R.S. M.G.S. &c. New Edition, in 1 thick vol. 8vo. illustrated with 1,241 Engravings on
Wood, £2. 10s. cloth lettered.

### A DICTIONARY OF PRACTICAL MEDICINE;
Comprising General Pathology, the Nature and Treatment of Diseases, Morbid Structures,
and the Disorders especially incidental to Climates, to Sex, and to the different Epochs of
Life, with numerous approved Formulæ of the Medicines recommended. By JAMES COPLAND,
M.D., Consulting Physician to Queen Charlotte's Lying-in Hospital; Senior Physician to the
Royal Infirmary for Children; Member of the Royal College of Physicians, London; of the
Medical and Chirurgical Societies of London and Berlin, &c. Publishing in parts, of which 7
have appeared.

### AN ENCYCLOPÆDIA OF COTTAGE, FARM, AND VILLA
ARCHITECTURE. With about 1,100 pages of Letterpress, and upwards of 2,000 Wood
Engravings; embracing designs of Cottages, Farm Houses, Farmeries, Villas, Country Inns,
Public Houses, Parochial Schools, &c.; including the interior Finishings and Furniture;
accompanied by Analytical and Critical Remarks illustrative of the Principles of Architectural
Science and Taste, on which the Designs for Dwellings are composed, and of Landscape
Gardening, with Reference to their Accompaniments. By J. C. LOUDON, F.L.S. &c. New
Edition, corrected, in 1 very thick vol. 8vo. with above 100 of the Plates re-engraved, contain-
ing above 100 entirely new illustrations, £3. 3s. handsomely bound in cloth, and lettered.

### THE FARMER'S ENCYCLOPÆDIA,
And DICTIONARY of RURAL AFFAIRS: embracing the most recent Discoveries in Agricultural Chemistry; adapted to the comprehension of unscientific Readers. By CUTHBERT
W. JOHNSON, Esq., Barrister at Law, Editor of the "Farmer's Almanack," &c. Illustrated
with Engravings of the most approved Agricultural Instruments. In 1 thick vol. 8vo. £2. 10s.
bound in cloth, and lettered. This work is published also in parts, at 5s. each, of which 9 have
appeared; to be completed in 1 more part.

### AN ENCYCLOPÆDIA OF ARCHITECTURE;
Historical, Theoretical, and Practical. By JOSEPH GWILT, Esq. F.S.A. In 1 thick vol. 8vo.
with numerous Illustrations on Wood. (In the Press.)

### AN ENCYCLOPÆDIA OF CIVIL ENGINEERING;
Historical, Theoretical, and Practical. By E. CRESY, Esq. F.A.S. C.E. In 1 thick vol. 8vo.
with numerous Illustrations on Wood. (Preparing for Publication.)

## V. JUVENILE WORKS.

### THE BOY'S COUNTRY BOOK:
Being the real Life of a Country Boy, written by himself; exhibiting all the Amusements,
Pleasures, and Pursuits of Children in the Country. Edited by WILLIAM HOWITT, Author
of "The Rural Life of England," &c. 2d Edition, 1 vol. fcp. 8vo. with about 40 Woodcuts,
8s. cloth.

### MASTERMAN READY;
Or, the Wreck of Pacific. Written for Young People. By CAPTAIN MARRYAT. 1 vol. fcp.
8vo. with numerous Engravings on Wood, 7s. 6d. cloth lettered.
Part 2 will be published in a few days.

### THE BOY'S OWN BOOK:
A Complete Encyclopædia of all the Diversions, Athletic, Scientific, and Recreative, of Boy-
hood and Youth. 19th Edition, Square, with numerous Engravings on Wood, 8s. 6d. boards.
CONTENTS.
Minor Sports; Games with Marbles; Games with Tops; Games with Balls; Sports of Agility
and Speed; Sports with Toys; Miscellaneous Sports; Athletic Sports; Archery, Cricket,
Gymnastics, Fencing; Aquatic Recreations; Angling, Swimming: The Fancier; Singing
Birds, Silkworms, Rabbits, Guinea Pigs, White Mice, Pigeons, Bantams: Scientific Recrea-
tions; Arithmetic, Magnetism, Optics, Aerostatics, Chemistry: Games of Skill; Draughts,
Chess: The Conjuror; Feats of Legerdemain, Tricks with Cards, Artificial Fireworks:
Miscellaneous Recreations; Deaf and Dumb Alphabet; Paradoxes and Puzzles, The Riddler,
Varieties.

### THE YOUNG LADIES' BOOK:
A Manual of Elegant Recreations, Exercises, and Pursuits. 4th Edition, with numerous
beautifully executed Engravings on Wood. £1. 1s. elegantly bound in crimson silk, lined with
imitation of Mechlin lace.
CONTENTS.
The Cabinet Council; L'Overture; Moral Deportment; the Florist; Mineralogy; Conchology;
Entomology; the Aviary; the Toilet; Embroidery; the Escritoir; Painting; Music;
Dancing; Archery; Riding; the Ornamental Artist; L'Adieu.

# VI. AGRICULTURE, FARMING, LAND-SURVEYING, &c.

## DESCRIPTIVE MEMOIRS AND ILLUSTRATIONS OF THE
BREEDS of the DOMESTIC ANIMALS of the BRITISH ISLANDS. By DAVID LOW, Esq. F.R.S.E., Professor of Agriculture in the University of Edinburgh. Imperial Quarto, Parts 1 to 13, (to be completed in 14 parts) 21s. each.

\*\*\* Each Part contains four beautifully coloured Plates, with a full History and Description of the Breeds contained in the Part.

" A beautifully illustrated work, which should be patronised by all the farmers' clubs.'—CUTHBERT W. JOHNSON.

The work is divided into four distinct divisions, as follows :—

1. The OX ; Five Parts and a Supplement, of which four are now published. This will comprise 22 Plates. The Supplement will be contained in Part 14 of the work.
2. The SHEEP; Five Parts and a Supplement, comprising 21 Plates. The Supplement will be contained in Part 14 of the work.
3. The HORSE; Two Parts (published), comprising 8 Plates.
4. The HOG ; One Part, with Supplement, comprising 5 Plates. The Supplement will be contained in Part 14 of the work.

## ELEMENTS OF PRACTICAL AGRICULTURE ;
Comprehending the Cultivation of Plants, the Husbandry of the Domestic Animals, and the Economy of the Farm. By DAVID LOW, Esq. F.R.S.E., Professor of Agriculture in the University of Edinburgh. 8vo. 3d Edition, with Alterations and Additions, with above 200 Woodcuts, 18s. cloth lettered.

## A TREATISE ON THE DOMESTIC ANIMALS ;
Comprehending their Food, Treatment, Breeding, Rearing, Diseases, &c. By PROFESSOR LOW. 1 vol. 8vo. (In the press.)

## LOUDON'S ENCYCLOPÆDIA OF AGRICULTURE.
(For particulars, see page 10 of Catalogue.)

## CUTHBERT JOHNSON'S FARMER'S ENCYCLOPÆDIA,
And Dictionary of Rural Affairs. (For particulars, see page 11 of Catalogue.)

## BAYLDON'S ART OF VALUING RENTS AND TILLAGES,
And the Tenant's Right of Entering and Quitting Farms, explained by several Specimens of Valuations; and Remarks on the Cultivation pursued on Soils in different Situations. Adapted to the Use of Landlords, Land-Agents, Appraisers, Farmers, and Tenants. 5th Edition, re-written and enlarged, by JOHN DONALDSON. With a Chapter on the Tithe-Commutation Rent-Charge, by a Gentleman of much experience on the Tithe Commission. 8vo. 10s. 6d. cloth lettered.

## TREATISE ON THE VALUATION OF PROPERTY FOR
THE POOR'S RATE ; showing the Method of Rating Lands, Buildings, Tithes, Mines, Woods, Navigable Rivers and Canals, and Personal Property : with an Abstract of the Poor Laws relating to Rates and Appeals. By J. S. BAYLDON, Author of "Rents and Tillages," 1 vol. 8vo. 7s. 6d. boards.

## SIR HUMPHRY DAVY'S AGRICULTURAL CHEMISTRY :
With Notes by Dr. JOHN DAVY. 6th Edition, 8vo. with 10 Plates, 16s. cloth lettered.

CONTENTS.

Introduction; The General Powers of Matter which Influence Vegetation; the Organization of Plants; Soils ; Nature and Constitution of the Atmosphere, and its Influence on Vegetables ; Manures of Vegetable and Animal Origin ; Manures of Mineral Origin, or Fossil Manures ; Improvement of Lands by Burning; Experiments on the Nutritive Qualities of different Grasses, &c.

## CROCKER'S ELEMENTS OF LAND SURVEYING.
Fifth Edition, corrected throughout, and considerably improved and modernized, by T. G. BUNT, Land Surveyor, Bristol. To which are added, TABLES OF SIX-FIGURE LOGARITHMS, &c., superintended by RICHARD FARLEY, of the Nautical Almanac Establishment. 1 vol. post 8vo. 12s. cloth lettered.

‡‡‡ The work throughout is entirely revised, and much new matter has been added ; there are new chapters, containing very full and minute Directions relating to the modern Practice of Surveying, both with and without the aid of angular instruments. The method of Plotting Estates, and Casting or Computing their Areas, are described, &c. &c. The chapter on Levelling also is new.

## OUTLINES OF A NEW PLAN OF TILLING AND FERTILIZING LAND. By THOMAS VAUX. 8vo. 6s. 6d. cloth lettered.

By the proposed system, all poor and waste lands (comprising one moiety of the United Kingdom), on which there are from four to five inches of soil, may be made to yield three times as much butcher's meat and wool per acre, as the richest grazing lands now yield ; effected principally by manual labour, and by tilling only one-fourth of the soil at a time ; and by that manure only which will be produced on the spot whereon the system is brought into operation.

# VII. GARDENING.

## LOUDON'S ENCYCLOPÆDIA OF GARDENING.
(For particulars, see page 10.)

## THE ROSE AMATEUR'S GUIDE:
Containing ample Descriptions of all the fine leading Varieties of Roses, regularly classed in their respective families; their History and Mode of Culture. By T. RIVERS, Jun. 2d Edition, with Alterations and Additions. 1 vol. fcp. 8vo. 6s. cloth lettered.

Among the additions to the present Edition will be found full Directions for Raising New Roses from Seed, by modes never before published, appended to each Family; with descriptions of the most remarkable New Roses lately introduced; an alphabetical list of all the New Roses and Show Flowers.

## THE VEGETABLE CULTIVATOR;
Containing a plain and accurate Description of all the different Species of Culinary Vegetables, with the most approved Method of Cultivating them by Natural and Artificial Means, and the best Modes of Cooking them; alphabetically arranged. Together with a Description of the Physical Herbs in General Use. Also, some Recollections of the Life of PHILIP MILLER, F.A.S., Gardener to the Worshipful Company of Apothecaries at Chelsea. By JOHN ROGERS, Author of "The Fruit Cultivator." Fcp. 8vo. 7s. cloth.

## A PRACTICAL TREATISE ON THE CULTIVATION OF THE
GRAPE VINE ON OPEN WALLS. By CLEMENT HOARE. 3d Edition, 8vo. 7s. 6d. cloth.
CONTENTS.
Introduction; Observations on the present Method of Cultivating Grape Vines on open Walls; on the capability and extent of the Fruit-bearing Powers of the Vine; on Aspect; on Soil; on Manure; on the Construction of Walls; on the Propagation of Vines; on the Pruning of Vines; on the Training of Vines; on the Management of a Vine during the first five years of its growth; Weekly Calendarial Register; General Autumnal Prunings; on the Winter Management of the Vine; on the Planting and Management of Vines in the public thoroughfares of towns; Descriptive Catalogue of twelve sorts of Grapes most suitably adapted for Culture on open Walls.

## PRACTICAL HINTS ON THE CULTURE OF THE PINE-
APPLE. By R. GLENDINNING, Gardener to the Right Hon. Lord Rolle, Bicton. 12mo. with Plan of a Pinery, 5s. cloth.

## THE THEORY OF HORTICULTURE;
Or, an Attempt to Explain the Principal Operations of Gardening upon Physiological Principles. By JOHN LINDLEY, Ph.D., F.R.S. 1 vol. 8vo. with Illustrations on Wood. 12s. cloth.

This book is written in the hope of providing the intelligent gardener, and the scientific amateur, correctly, with the rationalia of the more important operations of Horticulture; and the author has endeavoured to present to his readers an intelligible explanation, founded upon well ascertained facts, which they can judge of by their own means of observation, of the general nature of vegetable actions, and of the causes which, while they control the powers of life in plants, are capable of being regulated by themselves. The possession of such knowledge will necessarily teach them how to improve their methods of cultivation, and lead them to the discovery of new and better modes.

## AN OUTLINE OF THE FIRST PRINCIPLES OF HORTICUL-
TURE. By PROFESSOR LINDLEY. 18mo. 2s. sewed.

## A GUIDE TO THE ORCHARD AND KITCHEN GARDEN;
Or, an Account of the most valuable Fruits and Vegetables cultivated in Great Britain : with Kalendars of the Work required in the Orchard and Kitchen Garden during every month in the year. By GEORGE LINDLEY, C.M.H.S. Edited by PROFESSOR LINDLEY. 1 large vol. 8vo. 16s. boards.

## THE LANDSCAPE GARDENING AND LANDSCAPE ARCHI-
TECTURE of the late HUMPHRY REPTON, Esq.; being his entire works on these subjects. New Edition, with an historical and scientific Introduction, a systematic Analysis, a Biographical Notice, Notes, and a copious alphabetical Index. By J. C. LOUDON, F.L.S., &c. Originally published in 1 folio and 3 quarto volumes, and now comprised in 1 vol. 8vo. illustrated by upwards of 250 Engravings, and Portrait, 30s. cloth; with coloured plates £3. 6s. cloth.

## THE SUBURBAN GARDENER AND VILLA COMPANION :
Comprising the Choice of a Villa or Suburban Residence, or of a situation on which to form one; the Arrangement and Furnishing of the House; and the Laying-out, Planting, and general Management of the Garden and Grounds; the whole adapted for grounds from one perch to fifty acres and upwards in extent; intended for the instruction of those who know little of Gardening or Rural Affairs, and more particularly for the use of Ladies. By J. C. LOUDON, F.L.S., &c, 1 vol. 8vo. with above 300 Wood Engravings, 20s. cloth.

## A SELECTION FROM THE PHYSIOLOGICAL AND HORTI-
CULTURAL PAPERS, published in the Transactions of the Royal and Horticultural Societies, by the late T. A. KNIGHT, Esq., President of the Horticultural Society of London, &c. To which is prefixed a Sketch of his Life. 1 vol. royal 8vo. with Portrait and 7 Plates. 15s. cloth.

# VIII. MRS. MARCET'S WORKS.

## CONVERSATIONS ON CHEMISTRY;
In which the Elements of that Science are familiarly Explained and Illustrated by Experiments. 14th Edition, enlarged and corrected, 2 vols. fcp. 8vo. 14s. cloth.

## CONVERSATIONS ON NATURAL PHILOSOPHY;
In which the Elements of that Science are familiarly explained, and adapted to the comprehension of Young Persons. 9th Edition, enlarged and corrected by the Author. In 1 vol. fcp. 8vo. with 23 Plates, 10s. 6d. cloth.

CONTENTS.

Of the General Properties of Bodies; the Attraction of Gravity; the Laws of Motion; Compound Motion; the Mechanical Powers; Astronomy; Causes of the Earth's Motion; the Planets; the Earth; the Moon; Hydrostatics; the Mechanical Properties of Fluids; of Springs, Fountains, &c.; Pneumatics; the Mechanical Properties of Air; on Wind and Sound; Optics; the Visual Angle and the Reflection of Mirrors; on Refraction and Colours; on the Structure of the Eye, and Optical Instruments.

## CONVERSATIONS ON POLITICAL ECONOMY;
In which the Elements of that Science are familiarly explained. 7th Edition, revised and enlarged, 1 vol. fcp. 8vo. 7s. 6d. cloth.

CONTENTS.

Introduction; on Property; the Division of Labour; on Capital; on Wages and Population; on the Condition of the Poor; on Value and Price; on Income; Income from Landed Property; Income from the Cultivation of Land; Income from Capital lent; on Money; on Commerce; on Foreign Trade; on Expenditure and Consumption.

## CONVERSATIONS ON VEGETABLE PHYSIOLOGY;
Comprehending the Elements of Botany, with their application to Agriculture. 3d Edition, 1 vol. fcp. 8vo. with 4 Plates, 9s. cloth.

CONTENTS.

Introduction; on Roots; on Stems; on Leaves; on Sap; on Cambium and the peculiar Juices of Plants; on the Action of Light and Heat on Plants; on the Naturalization of Plants; on the Action of the Atmosphere on Plants; on the Action of Water on Plants; on the Artificial Mode of Watering Plants; on the Action of the Soil on Plants; on the Propagation of Plants by Subdivision; on Grafting; on the Multiplication of Plants by Seed; the Flower; on Compound Flowers; on Fruit; on the Seed; on the Classification of Plants; on Artificial Systems; on the Natural System; Botanical Geography; the Influence of Culture on Vegetation; on the Degeneration and Diseases of Plants; on the Cultivation of Trees; on the Cultivation of Plants which produce Fermented Liquors; on the Cultivation of Grasses, Tuberous Roots, and Grain; on Oleaginous Plants and Culinary Vegetables.

## CONVERSATIONS FOR CHILDREN;
On Land and Water. 2d Edition, revised and corrected, 1 vol. fcp. 8vo. with coloured Maps, showing the comparative altitude of Mountains, 5s. 6d. cloth lettered.

## JOHN HOPKINS' NOTIONS ON POLITICAL ECONOMY.
3d Edition, fcp. 8vo. 4s. 6d. cloth.

CONTENTS.

The Rich and the Poor, a fairy tale; Wages, a fairy tale; the Three Giants; Population, or the Old World; Emigration, or a New World; the Poor's Rate, or the Treacherous Friend; Machinery, or Cheap Goods and Dear Goods; Foreign Trade, or the Wedding Gown; the Corn Trade, or the Price of Bread.

\*\* A smaller Edition, in 18mo. 1s. 6d. sewed.

## MARY'S GRAMMAR;
Interspersed with Stories, and intended for the Use of Children. 5th Edition, revised and enlarged, 18mo. 3s. 6d. half-bound.

## WILLY'S HOLIDAYS;
Or, Conversations on Different Kinds of Governments, intended for Young Children. 18mo. 2s. half-bound.

CONTENTS.

How Willy gets into Debt; how the King has an Allowance like the School-boy; how the King gets into Debt like a School-boy; a curious way to pay Debts; Difference between making Laws and making people obey them; on Flogging Soldiers and School-boys; on Despotic Sovereigns; on Republics; on Slavery.

## WILLY'S STORIES FOR YOUNG CHILDREN.
Third Edition, 18mo. 2s. half-bound.

CONTENTS.

The House-building; the Three Pits (the Coal Pit, the Chalk Pit, and the Gravel Pit); and the Land without Laws.

## THE SEASONS;
Stories for very Young Children. 4 vols. 18mo. new Edition: Vol. 1, Winter; Vol. 2, Spring; Vol. 3, Summer; Vol. 4, Autumn. 2s. each volume, half-bound.